IRON ROADS

OF THE MONADNOCK REGION

Working upgrade at Troy Ledges, XW-2, the Bellows Falls-to-Worcester freight, has stepped onto the Gulf Bridge (B83.88) in Troy, NH. Though this image is undated, the completion of today's Rte. 12 (left) in 1945, and XW-2's last run with steam on Jan. 23, 1952, provide good bookends for a date range. Notice the old Keene Road, visible beneath the bridge. Photogr. Unknown; Carl R. Byron coll. (See more about Gulf Bridge inside on pages 70-71 and in Volume I, pages 97–98.)

IRON ROADS

OF THE MONADNOCK REGION

— VOLUME THREE - A PICTORIAL —

Railroads of Southwestern New Hampshire
and North-Central Massachusetts

by

Bradford G. Blodget and Richard R. Richards Jr.

BAUHAN PUBLISHING

PETERBOROUGH, NEW HAMPSHIRE

2023

This book is a selective history of the railroads in the Monadnock Region, focused on their operating years and their relationships to the communities they served. It is not intended to be a field guide to abandoned roadbeds and surviving railroad infrastructure and artifacts. Field exploration for such and the accompanying pleasures of discovery are reserved for the reader.

©2023 Historical Society of Cheshire County
ISBN 978-0-87233-368-0

Library of Congress Cataloging-in-Publication Data
Library of Congress Control Number: 2023935180
LC record available at https://lccn.loc.gov/2023935180

All photographs used by permission with credits in each caption.

Historical Society of Cheshire County
P.O. Box 803, 246 Main Street
Keene, New Hampshire 03431
WWW.HSCCNH.ORG

WWW.BAUHANPUBLISHING.COM

Book design by Henry James and Sarah Bauhan
Cover design by Henry James
Printed by Versa Press

FRONT COVER PHOTOGRAPH: Looking inward (timetable south) on the Keene Branch, above Keene in Marlboro, ca. 1910. In the day, the countryside was largely deforested. Sheep and cattle grazed the rough pasturage along the right-of-way and there were breathtaking views of Monadnock all along the south side of the railroad through Marlboro, Harrisville, and Hancock. But after 100 years of forest regrowth, the views are much diminished today. Postcard, Dr. L. G. Hildreth, publisher; Matthew D. Cosgro coll.

Printed in the United States of America

CONTENTS

PART ONE

PICTORIAL

PART TWO

PART THREE

FOREWORD

Railroad history is a place where geography, engineering, and sociology come together. In Volume III of *Iron Roads of the Monadnock Region*, Bradford G. Blodget and Richard R. Richards Jr. expand a series that educates readers about railroading in north-central Massachusetts and southern New Hampshire and Vermont. This new volume lets us partake of images not only from the sprawling Boston & Maine and its many antecedents, but also the Boston & Albany, the Central Vermont, and the interurban electric lines of this scenic country.

Volume III builds on a continuum that begins when the railroad formed the only connection of many rural towns to the outside world. It explores long-forgotten passenger routings from shady country stations and the switching of local paper and textile mills. Incredibly, freight service survived in some rural areas because the railroad was still the most economical way of getting raw materials in and finished products out. Where the railroad has persisted to the modern day, the *Iron Roads* timeline encompasses the regional roads that keep railroading alive.

Nothing brings a subject to life better than pictures. When combined with informative text and clear, well-drawn maps, the inspirational effect is powerful. A good railroad book can transport readers to a place they have never seen but put them right at home in the midst of switching, milk handling, snowplowing, and all the other tasks that are part and parcel of the railroad business. Railroad photography often concentrates on engines, but this book goes far beyond to show how the railroad, and its infrastructure and operations, changed the landscape and served the people who lived and worked in the Monadnock Region.

A good photo-oriented railroad book is also food for the imagination. Not only do the authors provide brain fodder for the modeler, they prompt general readers to investigate the history of their own geographical areas, or to delve into the archaeology of what the railroads left behind. Volume III illuminates a section of New England that has been underserved by railroad historians. Not surprisingly the varied terrain of the area demanded many engineering feats and curiosities that lent a picturesque quality to the railroading that happened there. Trestles, stone bridges, and earth-moving projects are all part of *Iron Roads*.

I first met Volume III lead author Brad Blodget several years ago when he became a fellow archives volunteer for the Boston & Maine Railroad Historical Society. It was obvious from the start that Brad enjoyed this volunteer activity, not only for the help he was giving our Society but also as a means of improving his own railroad knowledge. I attribute Brad's knack for identifying photographs to the attention to detail and the ability to ask questions and find answers that were necessary in his "real life" career as a scientist. He finds stories in the rich detail that lies hidden in the photos that would otherwise be enigmas to the casual browser.

So, pick up this book and be prepared for a very interesting trip.

—Frederick N. Nowell III, Archives Chairman
Boston & Maine Railroad Historical Society
January 2023

Jaffrey, NH, ca. 1970. The last passenger train departed Jaffrey March 7, 1953, the last freight train in 1984. The station building was painted white after the B&M sold the building in 1960. Prior to the sale, railroad had removed the order boards from the signal mast, but they were later reinstalled by persons interested in preserving the building's original features. Photogr. unknown; B.G. Blodget coll.

ACKNOWLEDGMENTS

We extend our most appreciative thanks to our sponsor, the Historical Society of Cheshire County, for its support, trust, and confidence in us for undertaking the *Iron Roads* project in the first place. Alan F. Rumrill, the Historical Society's director, and his supportive staff helped us with access to important resources and with myriad tasks. With our deepest gratitude we also remember and acknowledge the financial support received from a number of individual contributors that helped launch the *Iron Roads* project. We thank everyone who purchased copies of Volumes I and II. It was their collective support and positive response to the book that influenced the decision to proceed with the present volume.

The professional team at Bauhan Publishing in Peterborough, New Hampshire deserves a special salute. Sarah Bauhan, Henry James, and Mary Ann Faughnan were wonderful to work with and we simply cannot say enough good things about them.

We acknowledge with special gratitude the Boston & Maine Railroad Historical Society (B&MRRHS). Archivist Frederick N. Nowell III directed us to important photographic resources held by the Society. In addition, no fewer than twenty members of the Society—many of whom worked for the Boston & Maine Railroad—are among those listed below. Help came to us in many forms, from contributing images to helping us with captions, correcting us when we erred, supplying answers to technical matters and responding to our unending questions. The Boston & Maine Railroad's rich historical legacy lives on at the B&MRRHS and among its members.

We also wish to extend special thanks to several individuals who made major contributions of previously unpublished images for this pictorial. Stephan Frisiello, Archivist at the Walker Transportation Collection at Historic Beverly made available important historic railroad images from the Albert G. Hale and Donald S. Robinson collections, scans for which were supplied with the assistance of Bradford Kippen and Rick Kfoury. Benjamin Campbell shared with us his images and extensive knowledge of the Manchester & Keene Railroad. Larry Kemp, Richard E. Anderson, and Richard E. Miller shared many wonderful, unpublished images from their collections.

We appreciate material contributions to this volume from several local historical societies, including Ashburnham Historical Society, Hillsborough Historical Society, Historic Harrisville, Inc., Milford Historical Society, Narragansett Historical Society (Templeton, Massachusetts) and the Westminster (Massachusetts) Historical Society

In addition to those named above, we extend our thanks to the following individuals for their contributions, great and small: Harry Aldrich, the late Frederick G. Bailey, Carl R. Byron, the California State Railroad Museum Archives, Richard R. Conard, George C. Corey, Matthew D. Cosgro, Alden H. Dreyer, Jim Dufour, William A. Gleason, Erin Hammerstedt, Betsy Hannula, Wayne D. Hills, Richard K. Hurst, David S. Hutchinson, Richard F. Kowal, Leo Landry, Alan LePain, Alan E. MacMillan Jr., the late Brent S. Michiels, Dale Monette, Thomas Murray, Tom Pettee, Chris Pratt, Janice Roy, Dale O. Russell, Brian Tanguay, COL (Ret.) Tom E. Thompson, Harry L. York III, and Victor M. Zolinsky.

We thank Brian and Owen Boisvert/L. B. Wheaton's, Worcester, for help with scanning images; Bruce Davison for contributing his Photoshop skills; Samantha Gaucette at Keene State University for producing our route maps; and Adam Cole Barber of Art and Frame Emporium in Westborough, Massachusetts, and Isaac Perreault at Clark University in Worcester, for help with track diagrams.

In their glory years in the Monadnock Region, railroads were a wonderment, bringing connectivity to the wider world beyond. View of the Grand Monadnock from the cab of an E7 diesel, Feb. 26, 1951. George H. Hill photo; B&MRRHS Archives.

INTRODUCTION

In Volumes I and II of *Iron Roads of the Monadnock Region,* we presented in considerable detail, the histories of all the railroads—including street railways and quarry railroads—that operated in the Monadnock Region of southwestern New Hampshire and north-central Massachusetts from the 1840s. Mount Monadnock—the Grand Monadnock—in Jaffrey and Dublin, New Hampshire, dominates much of this area for miles around. Here, in Volume III, we present a pictorial of railroad operations in the Monadnock Region that is intended to complement and supplement Volumes I and II.

Although Volume III can be enjoyed as a standalone, all three volumes are written as an integrated whole. This third volume is divided into three parts. Part One includes our selections of images, arranged mostly in the chapter order we followed in Volumes I and II. Where appropriate, we stream images in station order outward from Boston, Worcester, or Springfield. At stations where we have multiple images, we've tried to keep them in roughly chronological order. We include thumbnail recaps and route maps of our subject roads to assist readers unfamiliar with the territory and who might not have had the benefit of reading the first two volumes. Part Two contains errata and addenda for the first two volumes. Part Three is an updated and consolidated index for all three volumes—providing the convenience of cross-referencing subject material appearing throughout the work.

Newfound photographic material has allowed us to augment the images we presented in the first two volumes—in some cases quite substantially. We would like to emphasize that the images we present in this pictorial are mostly newly discovered, not images that did not make the cut for Volumes I and II. We are living in a time when large collections of images taken in the 1930–1960 period are being dispersed by their owners or estates. The digitization of additional material, locked away for decades in known collections, is another tributary source of vintage images. The sheer volume of "new" images appearing is remarkable. That said, however, rail-

road images from the Monadnock Region per se are not particularly common. Trains were always scarcer there and the number of railfans and railroad enthusiast trips into the Region, far fewer.

To cite two examples, consider the Manchester & Keene Railroad. It was inherently difficult to follow, what with poor access—and the road's best years were long gone before anyone ever heard of a "railfan." In the late 1930s, railfans discovered the Cheshire Branch, where there were great photo opportunities. But the problem there was that one had to consult the timetable and plan ahead where they wanted to meet trains. They really had to know what they were doing. Chasing trains on the Cheshire was not practicable. Highway travel was slow, and the trains were faster then—fifty miles an hour on the Cheshire. We are fortunate that some skilled photographers persevered in the face of these difficulties and captured images we now treasure.

We have expanded our treatment of some of the more "peripheral" areas that we gave less attention to in Volumes I and II. For example, we focus more attention on the Vermont & Massachusetts Railroad—the main line demarcating the southern edge of the Monadnock Region. Also, we have added a completely new chapter to expand our original discussion of the Hillsboro Branch on the northeastern edge of the region. On the other hand, we have omitted chapters on the Sullivan County Railroad and the quarry roads because of a virtual absence of available photographic material.

One of the biggest challenges today is just visualizing the arrangement of railroad infrastructure at different localities, where so much is gone, including non-railroad landmarks. To address this, we have strived to both select images composed in good geographic contexts and to include as much "orientation detail" in our captions as possible, to help readers better visualize the way things looked in railroad days. After all, this is a pictorial, and we hope it will be a "being there" experience to the extent possible.

BOSTON & MAINE R.R.
At Greatest Extent — 1915
With Controlled Lines

EXPLANATION OF CONVENTIONS AND ABBREVIATIONS

Before we get started, we believe it would be helpful to briefly review certain railroad conventions followed and abbreviations used in Volumes I and II—and that we continue to use unchanged in Volume III.

In our captions, while we may sometimes use compass direction when describing the physical location of buildings or other features, we always use "timetable direction," as given in Boston & Maine Railroad (B&M) Employee Time Tables, when describing railroad operations. Beware, timetable directions are sometimes counterintuitive to compass directions! Also, in B&M parlance, trains—anywhere on the system—moving away from Boston, Worcester, or Springfield are referred to as *outward* trains, in the opposite direction as *inward* trains.

Thus, on the Vermont & Massachusetts (today's Fitchburg Main Line), trains traveling toward Millers Falls (Grouts) are outward/westward, toward Fitchburg inward/eastward. Cheshire Branch trains traveling toward Bellows Falls are outward/westward, toward South Ashburnham inward/eastward; Ashuelot Branch trains traveling toward Keene are outward/northward, toward East Northfield or Dole Junction inward/southward; Worcester & Contoocook trains moving toward Contoocook are outward/eastward, toward Worcester inward/westward; and trains on the Manchester & Keene (Keene Branch) traveling toward Keene are outward/northward, toward Nashua inward/southward. Also, for the Hillsboro Branch (which we did not discuss in detail in Volumes I and II), trains traveling toward Hillsboro are outward/northward, toward Nashua inward/southward.

Outward passenger trains carry odd numbers ("**Out**ward is **O**dd"), inward trains even numbers. Freight trains are designated by alphanumeric symbols ending in odd numbers for outward movements, even numbers for inward movements. Three examples of outward/inward symbols: WX-1/XW-2 for freights between Worcester and Bellows Falls, EK-1/KE-2 between East Northfield and Keene, and N-1/N-2 between Nashua and Hillsboro. For both specificity and brevity, we use these symbols in the text, explaining them upon their first appearances. Timetable directions and train numbers and symbols used by B&M predecessor roads may differ.

Decimalized numbers you may encounter in tables, timetables, or in the text following the names of stations, bridges, or signals, are B&M mileage points we have included for reference. For a linear enterprise like a railroad, spread out over a huge geographic area, mileages are critically important. They form a precision basis for maintaining an established order for everything from operations to rate-making. The mileages we use are generally taken from *B&M ETT No. 1*, effective April 29, 1928.

Mileages for the Fitchburg Route Main Line and Cheshire Branch are measured from the North Station bunters in Boston (B); for the Connecticut River Route Main Line from Springfield Union Station (S); for the Ashuelot Branch from either East Northfield (EN) or Springfield Union Station; for the Worcester and Contoocook line from Worcester Union Station (W); and for the Keene Branch and the Hillsboro Branch (1942–) from Nashua Union Station (N).

Before we launch into our chapters on individual roads, we present a few reference items concerning the Monadnock Region that show its position in broader geographic contexts.

(*opposite page*) Map of the Boston & Maine Railroad System at its maximum extent in 1915, courtesy of the B&MRRHS. Lines in the Monadnock Region are highlighted in red.

Abbreviated Railroad Names:
B&A—Boston & Albany;
BB&G—Boston, Barre & Gardner;
B&L—Boston & Lowell;
B&M—Boston & Maine;
CRRR—Connecticut River;
CV—Central Vermont;
M&K—Manchester & Keene;
N&L—Nashua & Lowell;
NYC—New York Central;
P&H—Peterborough & Hillsborough;
P&S—Peterborough & Shirley;
V&M—Vermont & Massachusetts;
W&C—Worcester & Contoocook

Abbreviated Street Railway Names:
A&O—Athol & Orange;
GW&F—Gardner, Westminster & Fitchburg;
KERy—Keene Electric;
NMSRy—Northern Massachusetts;
TSRy—Templeton

Other Abbreviations:
CTC—Centralized Traffic Control;
ETT and PTT—Employee and Public Time Tables;
MP—mile post or mileage point;
RDC—rail diesel car;
RRE—Railroad Enthusiasts, Inc.

Following railroad custom, we may use the shortened versions for Hillsborough, Marlborough, and Peterborough (omitting the "ugh") when the use of these names is directly connected to railroad operations.

(*opposite page*) Daily, dedicated milk train service in the Monadnock Region in 1898. All the milk train routes went to Boston, but which dairy company a country farmer could sell his milk to was determined by the railroad he happened to live on. For example, the Fitchburg Railroad brought milk picked up along its main line exclusively to the Boston Dairy Co. Connecting trains over the Cheshire and Worcester Branches set off cars for pickup. On the other hand, the Boston & Maine Railroad held the franchise for two different milk trains that picked up milk in the Monadnock Region for exclusive delivery to D. Whiting & Sons. One of these trains started from Keene, ran down the Ashuelot Branch to South Vernon, thence on the main line to Northampton, and finally over the Central Massachusetts Branch to Boston. The other train picked up milk along a route from Newport over the Claremont, the Worcester & Contoocook, and the Keene Branches. It connected at Elmwood with a milk train from Peterboro.

Numbers next to the stations appear to be the daily can numbers. While the map shows no milk trains were running at this time between Keene and Elmwood, that route did warrant a milk car (1887–1925) on the morning passenger train. In fact, on all lines, in addition to scheduled milk trains, smaller quantities of can milk moved in the baggage cars on passenger trains. (Map from Whitaker, George M. 1898. *The Milk Supply of Boston and other New England cities*, USDA, Washington.)

By 1930, changes were happening in the way milk was shipped. The railroads were moving away from handling can milk from hundreds of country milk stops, to the bulk movement of milk from creameries. Farmers would take their milk to a local creamery. The best-known creamery in the Monadnock Region was the Bellows Falls Co-operative Creamery. Opened in 1921, this creamery received milk from as many as 1,000 member farmers at its peak. Milk was bottled at the Creamery and moved on the B&M to Boston every night for almost forty-three years (see Vol. I, p. 73–76).

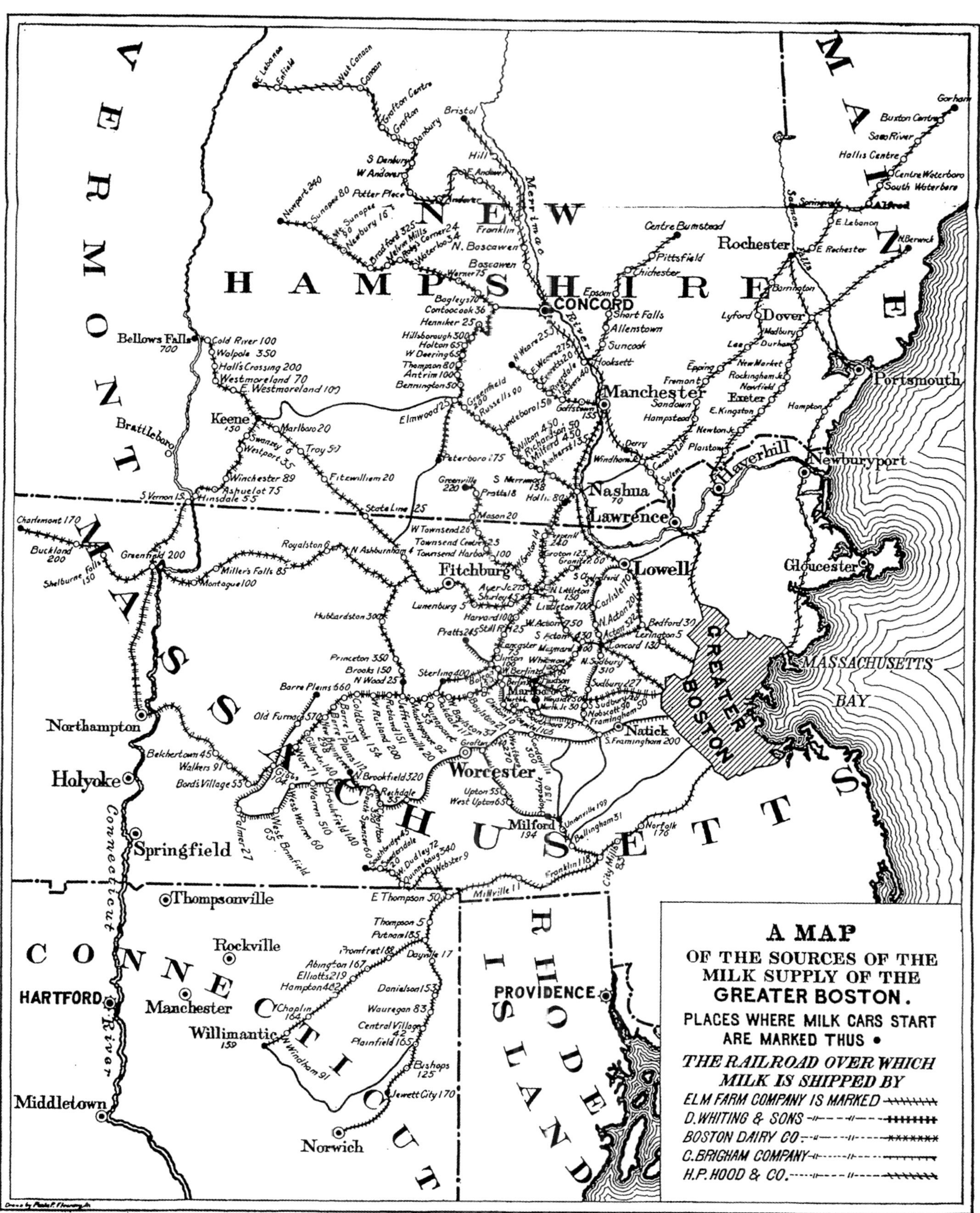

VERMONT
NEW HAMPSHIRE
MASSACHUSETTS
CONNECTICUT
RHODE ISLAND
MAINE
MASSACHUSETTS BAY
GREATER BOSTON
Connecticut River
Merrimac River
Bellows Falls
Brattleboro
Keene
Charlemont
Greenfield
Northampton
Holyoke
Springfield
Hartford
Middletown
Thompsonville
Rockville
Manchester
Willimantic
Norwich
Providence
Worcester
Fitchburg
Concord
Manchester
Nashua
Lawrence
Lowell
Natick
Milford
Franklin
Gloucester
Newburyport
Haverhill
Portsmouth
Dover
Rochester
Exeter
Bristol
Alfred
Gorham
A MAP
OF THE SOURCES OF THE
MILK SUPPLY OF THE
GREATER BOSTON.
PLACES WHERE MILK CARS START
ARE MARKED THUS •
THE RAILROAD OVER WHICH
MILK IS SHIPPED BY
ELM FARM COMPANY IS MARKED
D. WHITING & SONS
BOSTON DAIRY CO
C. BRIGHAM COMPANY
H. P. HOOD & CO.

Monadnock Region

79   Cheshire Branch: Boston-Keene-BellowsFalls-White River Jct.

Northbound — Boston to Bellows Falls

Miles	Northbound		51-5501 exSun AM	5551 Sun AM	Bus Sat. AM	Green Mt 5503 Daily AM	5507 exSun PM	Cheshire ◆5505u Mon-Fri PM	Monad-nock 5509 Daily PM	Cheshire ◆5555u Sun PM	Mount Royal 5511 exSun PM	5557 Sun PM
0.0	BOSTON (No. Sta.)......Mass.	Lv	2 15	....	a8 00	9 00	3 00	4 10	5 10	6 15	7 45	8 05
3.4	Cambridge		...	...	b8 08	9 08	3 08	Mon	v5 18	....	7 53	8 13
9.9	Waltham		2 33	....	....	9 19	3 19	to	....	....	8 02	8 23
36.1	Ayer		3 23	...	9 20	9 53	3 57	Fri	5 57	....	8 40	8 58
49.6	Fitchburg	Ar	3 50	....	....	10 13	4 19	inc.	6 15	....	8 58	9 16
49.6	Fitchburg	Lv	4 25	5 05	9 50	10 17	4 25	v5 06	6 20	v7 11	9 05	9 20
59.9	South Ashburnham		4 44	5 23	δ10 10	f10 36	4 44	....	....	....	....	....
67.9	WINCHENDON	Ar	4 54	5 33	....	10 46	4 54	5 29	....	....	9 35	9 50
67.9	WINCHENDON	Lv	5 10	5 45	10 30	10 50	4 58	5 34	e6 52	7 35	9 40	9 55
70.9	State Line......N.H.		f5 15	f5 50	....	....	5 11	stream-	f7 05	....	e9 52	e10 07
76.3	Fitzwilliam		5 24	5 57	c10 46	11 03	5 28	line	f7 14	....	10 01	f10 16
81.6	Troy		5 33	6 11	d10 55	11 12	f5 34	train	...	...	...	...
85.3	Webb		f5 38	f6 17	...	...	...	...	...	...	...	...
91.3	KEENE		6 03	6 35	11 20	11 32	5 50	6 06	7 33	8 08	10 25	10 40
100.4	Gilboa		f6 20	f6 52	...	...	f6 07	...	...	...	...	...
103.7	Westmoreland		6 26	6 58	g11 43	....	...	...	...	...	...	...
109.8	Walpole		6 36	7 08	g11 55	12 02	6 36	...	e8 03	...	e10 57	...
113.8	Bellows Falls......Vt.	Ar	6 45	7 17	12 05	12 10	6 45	6 37	8 10	8 40	11 05	11 20

Northbound — Bellows Falls to White River Jct.

Miles	Northbound		703 exSun AM	73 exSun PM	77 Sun PM	717 exSun PM	◆5505u PM	5555u PM	79 exSun AM	7059 Sun AM
113.8	BELLOWS FALLS......Vt.	Lv	7 08	12 48	2 48	7 00	6 37	8 40	11 32	11 33
120.9	Charlestown......N.H.	Ar	7 20	1 01	3 01	7 14	6 51	8 54	11 44	11 44
	Springfield (Vt. Trans. Co.) Vt.	Ar	....	....	4 40	7 45	7 45	....	....	....
131.0	Claremont Jct......N. H.		7 33	1 16	3 16	7 29	7 03	9 08	11 59	11 59
138.9	Windsor......Vt.		7 48	1 34	3 28	7 46	7 13	9 18	12 15	12 16
153.0	WHITE RIVER JCT.	Ar	8 10	2 05	3 50	8 25	7 35	9 40	12 45	12 45

Southbound — White River Jct. to Bellows Falls

Southbound		AM	78 exSun AM	◆5506u exSun AM	AM	AM	72 exSun PM	74 Sun PM	74 exSun PM
WHITE RIVER JCT......Vt.	Lv	....	4 00	7 00	....	....	12 15	2 50	2 50
Windsor		....	4 23	7 22	...	...	12 41	3 12	3 12
Claremont Jct......N. H.		....	4 40	7 32	....	....	12 55	3 33	3 33
Springfield (Vt. Trans. Co.) Vt.	Lv	....	...	7 15	...	...	11 30	...	...
Charlestown......N. H.		....	f4 54	7 45	....	....	1 11	3 46	3 46
Bellows Falls......Vt.	Ar	....	5 06	8 00	...	...	1 22	3 57	3 57

Southbound — Bellows Falls to Boston

Southbound		Mt Royal 5502 Daily AM	5504 exSun AM	Cheshire ◆5506u AM	5550 Sun AM	Bus Sat. AM	5508 exSun PM	Green Mt 5512 Sun PM	5510 exSun PM
BELLOWS FALLS......Vt.	Lv	4 50	6 55	8 00	9 40	12 45	1 35	4 05	4 05
Walpole......N. H.		....	v7 02	streamline	9 47	g12 58	f1 42	....	4 12
Westmoreland		....	7 12	train	...	g1 10	...	...	...
Gilboa		....	....	....	....	....	....	....	....
KEENE		5 31	7 38	8 31	10 18	1 34	2 15	4 44	4 46
Webb		....	....	....	....	....	....	....	....
Troy		v5 50	7 55	....	f10 35	d1 51	2 34	f5 01	5 05
Fitzwilliam		6 00	8 05	....	10 44	c2 01	2 44	f5 11	5 15
State Line		...	f8 13	...	...	...	2 56	5 25	5 27
WINCHENDON......Mass.	Ar	....	....	....	....	....	....	....	....
WINCHENDON......Mass.	Lv	6 14	8 23	9 03	11 05	2 20	3 00	5 25	5 31
South Ashburnham	Ar	f6 27	8 35	....	11 15	δ2 40	3 13	....	....
Fitchburg	Ar	6 42	8 48	e9 27	11 28	2 55	3 26	5 51	5 55
Fitchburg	Lv	7 06	8 55	....	11 42	....	3 32	5 51	6 01
Ayer	Ar	7 30	9 16	...	12 00	3 25	3 57	...	6 18
Waltham		8 27	9 57	....	12 37	....	4 54	6 37	6 52
Cambridge		8 37	10 07	e10 17	12 47	b4 40	5 07	6 47	7 06
BOSTON (No. Sta.)	Ar	8 45	10 15	10 25	12 55	a4 50	5 15	6 55	7 15

Reference marks:

a   Bus stop Park Square.
b   Bus stop Kendall Square.
c   Bus stop Highway.
d   Bus stop Square.
e   Stops to discharge passengers.
f   Stops on signal to discharge or receive.
g   Bus stop Post Office.
k   Saturdays only.
t   Coach passengers change on arrival at New Haven and Springfield.
u   No checked baggage handled on this train.
v   Stops only to receive passengers.
◆   "The Cheshire" Streamline train is limited in equipment and will receive passengers only to the extent of its capacity. All seats are reserved and assigned in advance. All coach class tickets honored except that those for restricted excursions will not be valid. No checked baggage handled on this train. No skis or other winter sports equipment will be accepted. Buffet service.
‡   Except Saturdays.
✠   Will not run on any holidays listed below.
□   Will not run Nov. 27, Dec. 25, Jan. 1.
δ   This time is at Ashburnham.
Bus Motor Coach.
Holidays: Oct. 13, Nov. 11, Nov. 27, Dec. 25, Jan. 1, Feb. 23, April 19.

1947 Calendar

	SUN	MON	TUE	WED	THU	FRI	SAT
JAN.				1	2	3	4
	5	6	7	8	9	10	11
	12	13	14	15	16	17	18
	19	20	21	22	23	24	25
	26	27	28	29	30	31	
FEB.							1
	2	3	4	5	6	7	8
	9	10	11	12	13	14	15
	16	17	18	19	20	21	22
	23	24	25	26	27	28	
MAR.							1
	2	3	4	5	6	7	8
	9	10	11	12	13	14	15
	16	17	18	19	20	21	22
	23	24	25	26	27	28	29
	30	31					
APR.			1	2	3	4	5
	6	7	8	9	10	11	12
	13	14	15	16	17	18	19
	20	21	22	23	24	25	26
	27	28	29	30			
MAY					1	2	3
	4	5	6	7	8	9	10
	11	12	13	14	15	16	17
	18	19	20	21	22	23	24
	25	26	27	28	29	30	31
JUNE	1	2	3	4	5	6	7
	8	9	10	11	12	13	14
	15	16	17	18	19	20	21
	22	23	24	25	26	27	28
	29	30					
JULY			1	2	3	4	5
	6	7	8	9	10	11	12
	13	14	15	16	17	18	19
	20	21	22	23	24	25	26
	27	28	29	30	31		
AUG.						1	2
	3	4	5	6	7	8	9
	10	11	12	13	14	15	16
	17	18	19	20	21	22	23
	24	25	26	27	28	29	30
	31						
SEP.		1	2	3	4	5	6
	7	8	9	10	11	12	13
	14	15	16	17	18	19	20
	21	22	23	24	25	26	27
	28	29	30				
OCT.				1	2	3	4
	5	6	7	8	9	10	11
	12	13	14	15	16	17	18
	19	20	21	22	23	24	25
	26	27	28	29	30	31	
NOV.							1
	2	3	4	5	6	7	8
	9	10	11	12	13	14	15
	16	17	18	19	20	21	22
	23	24	25	26	27	28	29
	30						
DEC.		1	2	3	4	5	6
	7	8	9	10	11	12	13
	14	15	16	17	18	19	20
	21	22	23	24	25	26	27
	28	29	30	31			

80   Worcester-Peterboro

Miles	Sun 8159 AM	exSun 8111 AM	READ DOWN	READ UP	exSun 8118 PM	Sun 8164 PM
0.0	9 20	9 00	Lv WORCESTER(U.Sta.)....Ar		4 40	6 50
0.8	9 23	9 03	...Lincoln Square...Mass...Lv		4 36	6 47
3.0			......Barber...... ..		f4 30	
8.3	f9 38	f9 19	...Holden ..		4 19	f6 31
9.5	v9 41	9 22	...Jefferson ..		4 15	f6 28
13.1	e9 48	e9 29	...Brooks ..		v4 07	v6 21
15.9	f9 56	9 38	...Princeton ..		4 00	f6 15
20.0	10 05	9 48	...Hubbardston ..		3 52	f6 07
26.2	10 17	10 00	Ar GARDNER .. Lv		3 40	5 55
....	8 10	8 30	Lv Boston (No. Sta.) .. Ar		5 30	8 20
26.2	10 21	10 15	Lv GARDNER .. Ar		3 30	5 55
27.2	10 24	10 18	...Heywood .. Lv		3 26	5 50
32.4	f10 34		...Red School ..			
36.0	10 45	10 39	Ar WINCHENDON .. Lv		3 05	5 30
....	9 00	9 00	Lv Boston (No. Sta.) ..Ar		5 15	6 55
36.0	10 53	10 53	Lv WINCHENDON.. Lv		2 52	5 17
39.7	...	...	...Rand .. N.H. Lv		...	...
40.6	...	f11 05	...Wetmore (Thomas) ..			...
41.8	f11 10	11 10	...West Rindge ..		2 38	f5 02
45.4	11 18	11 20	...East Jaffrey ..		2 29	4 54
48.0	...		...Hadley		f4 46	
49.4		f11 31	...Drury		f2 13	
50.5	v11 34		...Noone		e2 09	f4 39
51.9	11 35	11 38	Ar PETERBORO .. Lv		2 05	4 35

Ashuelot Branch   81

Miles	Rail-road	Sun PM	exSun PM	exSun AM	Sun AM	READ DOWN	READ UP	Sun AM	exSun PM	exSun PM	Sun PM
0.0	N. H.	12 30	12 30	4 45	12 10	Lv New York G.C.T.....N.Y. Ar			4 10	10 05	10 05
55.6	..	1 41	1 41	6 25	1 44	...Bridgeport ...Conn.			2 50	8 46	8 46
72.3	..	2 05	2 05	t6 55	2 20	...New Haven ..			2 25	8 20	8 20
108.9	..	3 08	3 08	8 00	3 45	...Hartford .. Ar			1 27	7 17	7 17
134.3	..	3 43	3 43	t8 42	4 23	Ar Springfield....Mass. Lv			12 55	6 45	6 45
		7055	**717**	**73**	**7051**			**712**	**74**	**74**	
0.0	B&M	4 00	4 00	9 30	4 55	Lv Springfield....Mass. Ar			12 30	6 23	6 23
49.7	..	5 34	5 39	11 37	6 07	Ar East Northfield Lv			10 50	4 57	4 57
		7353	**7305**	**7301**	**7351**			**7350**	**7300**	**7302**	**7302**
49.7	..	5 37	5 52	11 49	9 45	Lv E. NORTHFIELD .. Ar		9 34	10 34	4 44	4 44
51.9	..	f5 42	f5 58	f11 54	f9 50	...Dole Jct. ...N. H. ..		9 29	10 29	4 39	4 39
54.5	..	f5 48	6 04	12 00	f9 56	...Hinsdale ..		f9 20	10 20	4 30	f4 30
58.0	..	f5 56	6 12	12 08	f10 04	...Ashuelot ..		f9 12	10 12	4 22	f4 22
60.2	..	f6 02	6 18	12 14	f10 10	...Winchester ..		9 07	10 07	4 16	f4 16
65.6	..	f6 12	f6 28	f12 25	f10 20	...Westport ..		f8 57	f9 57	4 05	f4 05
68.2	..	f6 18	6 34	12 31	f10 26	...West Swanzey ..		f8 52	9 52	3 59	f3 59
70.4	..			f12 36	f10 31	...Swanzey ..				3 53	f3 53
73.7	..	6 30	6 46	12 45	10 40	Ar KEENE .. Lv		8 40	9 40	3 45	3 45

Passenger train service in the Monadnock Region shown in the *B&M PTT* dated Sept. 28, 1947. The timetable shows many of the train numbers we use in our captions

PART I

CHAPTER ONE

THE VERMONT & MASSACHUSETTS RAILROAD
The "Hoosac Tunnel Route"

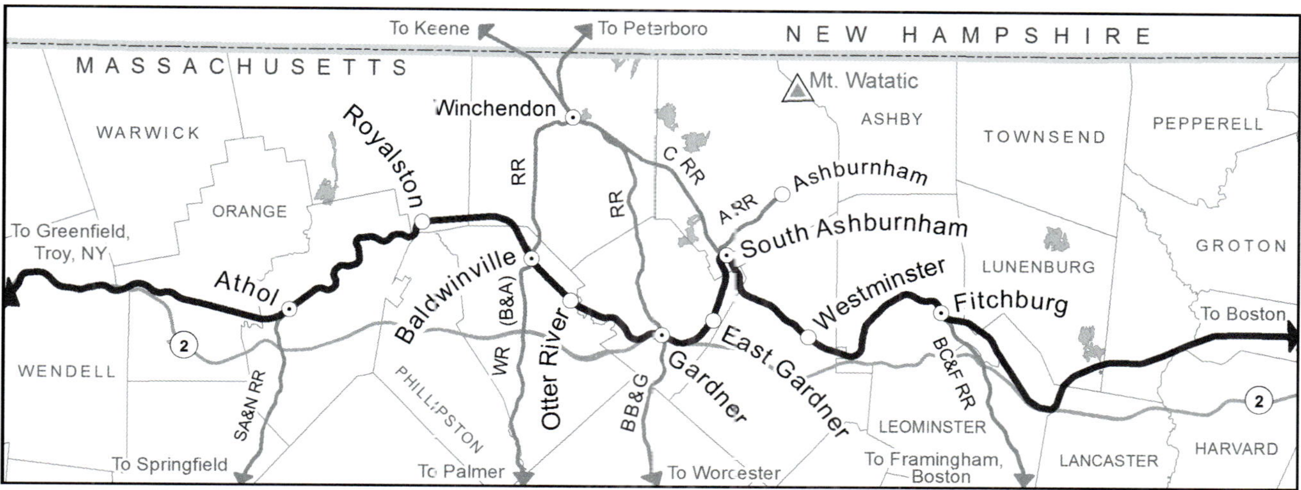

The Vermont & Massachusetts Railroad (V&M), with the backing of Fitchburg paper magnate Alvah Crocker and the Fitchburg Railroad, was chartered in Massachusetts on March 15, 1844. It was constructed in 1843–1849 between Fitchburg and Grouts Corner (Millers Falls), where it made a right-angle turn and continued north to the Vermont border. Under a Vermont charter, it was completed to Brattleboro in 1851. In 1850, an eight-mile extension was built from Grouts Corner to Greenfield, and this would eventually become a part of the main line westward to the Hudson Valley following the Hoosac Tunnel's opening in 1875. The line from Grouts to Brattleboro was sold to the New London Northern Railroad in 1880.

The V&M was the first railroad to lay iron in the Monadnock Region. The road ascended and crossed the southern extension of the Monadnock Plateau—the Worcester Plateau in north-central Massachusetts—from Westminster to Athol, forming the southern border of the Monadnock Region. Although this section of the road was only 26.9 miles in length, it was an integral part of the larger road and was the root from which three other railroads built further north into the very heart of the Monadnock Region. The Cheshire left the V&M at South Ashburnham to reach Bellows Falls via Keene. The Boston, Barre & Gardner (BB&G), successors to which would later form a part of the Worcester & Contoocook route to Winchendon, Peterborough, Elmwood, and Hillsboro, crossed the road at Gardner. The Ware River Railroad crossed the road at Baldwinville and reached northward as far as Winchendon. The Springfield, Athol & Northeastern reached the V&M at Athol, but never extended further. The latter two roads—late the Boston & Albany's Winchendon and Athol Branches—had both dreamed in their early years of invading New Hampshire, but such never happened. The tiny Ashburnham Railroad may also have been one of the dreamers. All these roads, of course, had their sights fixed on reaching the industrialized Merrimack Valley.

As an independent road, the V&M was never very profitable. Its construction costs had drastically exceeded projections and traffic growth was anemic. In its rush to open, the road had been built as inexpensively as possible. After struggling in its early years, the V&M leased itself for 999 years to the Fitchburg Railroad, beginning January 1, 1874. The Fitchburg was, in turn, leased by the Boston & Maine (B&M) July 1, 1900.

The V&M was originally built with 56-pound rail as a single track, unsignalized, east–west road, with passing sidings at all stations. There were fifty-seven bridges twenty-five feet or more in length, aggregating to over 6,000 feet. Thirty-one bridges were Howe covered wooden truss bridges, the remainder masonry. The road's highest elevation was 1,112 feet, reached at East Gardner (MP62.14). Westward from Fitchburg to the summit, the road rises 672 feet in 12.59 miles; eastward from Athol to the summit, 571 feet in 19.76 miles.

The Fitchburg and the B&M, successors to the V&M, spent years strengthening, rebuilding, and modernizing their "Fitchburg Main Line." A switchback at South Ashburnham was replaced by a horseshoe curve in 1876–1877, decrepit wooden stations were rebuilt, iron rails upgraded to steel, and bridges ironized. The road was mostly double-tracked by 1886 and was deep-rock ballasted in the 1920s. An Automatic Block Signal System was installed in 1908–1910, followed by Automatic Train Stop in 1926. In 1930, a Centralized Traffic Control System was installed—one of the earliest and largest systems of its kind in the world at the time. The Main Line was completely dieselized by the end of 1946.

The B&M was acquired by Guilford Rail Systems on June 30, 1983. Guilford rebranded itself Pan Am Railway in 2006 and in 2008 formed a 50-50 joint venture with Norfolk Southern Railway—Pan Am Southern, LLC—to own and operate the 155-mile, former V&M/Fitchburg/B&M Main Line between Ayer and Mechanicville, New York. On June 1, 2022, CSX Corporation purchased Pan Am Railway, including its 50 percent ownership of Pan Am Southern, LLC. The V&M still exists on paper as a real property-holding, corporate entity within CSX.

Much of the V&M was built through some challenging territory. Even today, much of the road's course across northern Massachusetts—through deep forests and the Millers River Valley—is nearly as wild, remote, and inaccessible as it was fifty years ago. This is not a side-of-the-highway railroad. Improvements over the years to Route 2 have only marginally improved the line's accessibility. As has always been the case, most railroad photography along the road has been at stations, where the line touches civilization.

Except for a small piece of the Connecticut River Main Line and a fragment of the old Cheshire in Walpole, New Hampshire, Pan Am Southern's main line across north-central Massachusetts is the only large stretch of active railroad remaining in the Monadnock Region. The original V&M lives on.

South Ashburnham (MP B59.90)

1-1. Boston–Mechanicville BM-1, drawn by Mountain 4109 is climbing Ashburnham Hill, "about a half-mile southwest of South Ashburnham," Sept. 7, 1941. The Mountains (4-8-2s), built by Baldwin, were the heaviest steam engines the B&M ever purchased and were restricted to the main lines. Chronically power-short before the outbreak of World War II, the B&M received them just in time to help handle the coming surge of wartime tonnage. Railroad photography was restricted during the war and pictures of these engines working are not overly common. Albert G. Hale photo; Walker Trans. Coll./ Historic Beverly.

Gardner (MP B64.66)

1-2. This 1875 stereo card image shows the Fitchburg's old V&M station at Gardner (see also Vol. I, page 39). The station became seriously outmoded before the Fitchburg finally got around to replacing it with the brick station that adjoined its Worcester Branch (former BB&G) station in 1896. T. Lewis, publisher; L. Hietala coll.

1-3. Gardner station at the crossing of the Worcester & Contoocook, looking eastward on the B&M Fitchburg Main Line. At right is the pulley-operated ball signal that, from V&M days, protected the diamond here. One ball displayed gave Worcester & Contoocook trains rights across the diamond. A Peterboro, possibly Concord-bound train, has cleared the diamond and is stopped in the station, ca. 1905. Postcard; B. G. Blodget coll.

1-4. Boston–to–Troy, NY, Train 55 in the station at Gardner. Note the big chair—said to be the largest in the world—on the station lawn. Chair making was a huge industry in the Monadnock Region in the first half of the twentieth century. Feb. 12, 1927. Carlton Parker photo; Richard E. Miller coll.

1-5. Train 55 *Berkshire Flyer*, Pacific 3669, in the station at Gardner. Notice, at the time this image was taken, the non-CTC interlocking signals were still in place, indicating the new CTC system was still incomplete, April 20, 1931. Photogr. unknown; B. G. Blodget coll.

1-6. Gardner Tower as it appeared in 1929, shortly before the advent of Centralized Traffic Control (CTC). Gardner Tower is the building between the water tank and the station. In railroad parlance, a "tower" is a railroad building in which an operator, by controlling switches and signals, directs train movements. Gardner Tower was the only B&M standard plan tower in the Monadnock Region. It was an all-mechanical lever tower until 1915, when a powered Union Switch & Signal double-arm, lower quadrant, Style B, Automatic Block Signal (ABS) System was activated to control traffic on the Fitchburg Division Main Line. With ABS, electric motors, activated by track circuitry, moved the signal blades. Some tower-operated, all-mechanical signals and switches which were not included in the ABS System remained and would continue in use. Photogr. unkown.

1-7. Inside Gardner Tower was a 56-lever mechanical switching plant. Since we were unable to locate an image showing the bank of levers inside Gardner Tower, we substitute this view inside the Manchester, New Hampshire Tower. Both were B&M standard plan towers. The "armstrong" levers were connected to rods (inside pipes) that ran alongside the tracks to reach switches and signals, allowing towermen to control them remotely. Some of the levers were easy to move, but others were balky—particularly those for switches farthest from the tower. Experienced towermen knew the idiosyncrasies of each lever and the "tricks" to move them. Out in the yard, the pipes were a dangerous trip hazard, especially in the dark of night or when buried in snow. In the image, William H. Marshall is pulling the last lever in the tower, before the cut-over to a modern, electric, interlocking signal system in the Manchester yards, Dec. 1, 1944. George H. Hill photo; B&MRRHS Archives.

In 1930, Centralized Traffic Control (CTC) was installed between a point about 1,500 feet west of Westminster to a point (Tyter West) about 2,800 feet east of Orange, a distance of about twenty-eight miles. The system was activated west of a point about 5,000 feet west of Gardner on June 15, 1931, and east of that point on July 19, 1931 (*B&M Fitchburg Div. Bull.* Order Nos. 103 and 129, dated June 8 and July 10, 1931, respectively). The system, under the direction of the train dispatcher at Gardner Tower, controlled switches and signals at twelve different interlocking plants between Westminster and Tyter West. It was not one continuous interlocking plant. The twelve interlocking plants were, from east to west: Westminster, South Ashburnham, East Gardner, Gardner (East), Gardner, Parker, Baldwinville (East), Baldwinville, Wright's Crossover, Athol, Tyter East, and Tyter West.

The Depression apparently slowed work and the CTC installation at Gardner Tower remained incomplete. Thus, the tower's old lever plant—for non-CTC interlockings—would continue in use alongside the CTC machine until December 24, 1934, when remaining tower-controlled switches were either incorporated into the CTC system or converted to hand-thrown switches.

The Tyter West CTC interlocking plant was retired March 6, 1958. Then, in 1967–1969, all remaining CTC interlockings controlled from Gardner were either retired or their control transferred to Greenfield. The last to go were Gardner (East), Gardner, and Parker, for which control was transferred to Greenfield.

1-7A. This is a towerman's perspective of the Peterboro Branch crossing diamonds on the B&M's Fitchburg Main Line. After crossing the diamonds, westbound Peterboro Branch trains continued right through the middle of the Worcester Yard. Notice the five-track Conant St. crossing that appears to have been protected by one flagman—and no gates! The corner of the passenger station and platform is at left. On the main line, note the CTC color light signals and the Railway Express Agency (REA) Building across the tracks from the station, Gardner, ca. 1942. The 1961-63 construction of the Rte. 2 embankment obliterated the Worcester Yard and radically transformed the surrounding landscape. See Chapter 10 for more images of the old Worcester Yard. Marium E. Foster photo; Hist. Soc. Cheshire Cty.

1-8. It was a different time. Hats and heavy woolen overcoats were the order of the day. Early in the morning of this day, the B&M had taken delivery of streamline train 6000 at its western gateway in Mechanicville, N.Y. and the train had been sent east on its maiden trip on the B&M over the Main Line to Boston. The Publicity Dept. had advertised stops along the route at North Adams, Greenfield, Gardner, and Fitchburg to allow the public to inspect the train—the first streamliner anywhere in the East. Over 9,000 people were able to go through the train, while hundreds more were reportedly turned away at all stops due to time limitations. Railroad officials hoped that improved and inspiring trains would win back traffic being lost to automobiles. What kind of a railroad event could possibly cause such palpable excitement today? This image shows the huge crowd surrounding the train at Gardner, Saturday, Feb. 9, 1935. Photogr. unknown.

Timetable for Tomorrow

Where to see the new streamlined "Flying Yankee" 'tomorrow:

Leaves Mechanicville, N Y	7:00 a m
Passes Johnsonville, N Y	7:25 a m
Passes Eagle Bridge, N Y	7:38 a m
Passes Hoosick Falls, N Y	7:48 a m
Passes Williamstown, Mass	8:25 a m
Arrives North Adams	8:35 a m
Exhibit to public....8:45 a m to	10:15 a m
Leaves North Adams	10:30 a m
Passes Shelburne Falls	11:20 a m
Arrives Greenfield	11:40 a m
Exhibit to public..11:45 a m to	1:30 p m
Leaves Greenfield	1:40 p m
Passes Orange	2:15 p m
Passes Athol	2:25 p m
Arrives Gardner	2:55 p m
Exhibit to public......3 p m to	3:45 p m
Leaves Gardner	3:55 p m
Arrives Fitchburg	4:25 p m
Exhibit to public...4:30 p m to	5:30 p m
Leaves Fitchburg	5:40 p m
Passes Shirley	5:49 p m
Passes Ayer	5:55 p m
Passes Littleton	5:59 p m
Passes West Acton	6:04 p m
Passes South Acton	6:06 p m
Passes Concord	6:12 p m
Passes Lincoln	6:16 p m
Passes Waltham	6:24 p m
Passes Waverley	6:27 p m
Passes Belmont	6:28 p m
Passes Cambridge	6:31 p m
Arrives North Station	6:40 p m

1-9. Gardner looking west along the main line. Note the Peterboro Branch diamonds, the three-light CTC color light signal at the station, the tower with its two orderboard masts, and the water tank and section house. The long string of boxcars spotted at the freight house reflect how important Gardner once was as a (furniture) shipping point on the B&M. Oct. 15, 1948. Albert G. Hale photo; Walker Trans. Coll./Historic Beverly.

1-10. Gardner looking east toward the old South Main St. Bridge. In the foreground is the Gardner Tower, July 16, 1949. Alan Thomas photo; B. G. Blodget coll.

1-11. Train 55, now a B&M "Highliner," making its station stop at Gardner, ca. 1953. George H. Hill photo; B&MRRHS Archives.

1-12. Images of GE 44-tonners working in Gardner are uncommon, but here is one showing a 44-tonner by the tower, ca. 1956. Photogr. unknown; Richard E. Miller coll.

1-13. There's nothing like a good mystery and this image, taken from the old South Main St. Bridge in Gardner, certainly fits the bill. It's an unexplained westbound train—with New Haven coaches—stopped at the station, where there is a sizeable crowd on the platform, ca. 1956. Nobody seems to know what this train was doing in Gardner. Mystery aside, the view from the bridge is interesting. Note Conant St. at left and the REA Building—looking unused—across the tracks from the station. The station would be razed in Oct. 1959. All the structures in the image, as well as the bridge the photographer was standing on, are gone today. Photogr. unknown; B. G. Blodget coll.

1-14. Gardner Yard looking east from the Mechanic St. crossing, Oct. 1959. In 1961–1963, construction of the Rte. 2 embankment cut Mechanic St. in two and buried everything you see to the right of the tracks. The grain elevator disappeared in a ball of fire in the early 1970s. Photogr. unknown; B&MRRHS Archives.

1-15. This view is from the Worcester Yard, looking timetable eastward on the Worcester & Contoocook. Directly ahead is the Conant St. crossing and the Peterboro Branch diamonds. Gardner Tower is at left center and Gardner station (being demolished) to the right. 1959. See more Worcester Yard images in Chapter 10. Photogr. unknown; B&MRRHS Archives.

1-16. All the wooden, outside-braced boxcars—the quintessential way cars that once wandered the B&M system—were withdrawn from service prior to May 15, 1966. Here we see Rigby to Mechanicville freight RM-3 passing Gardner Tower with some of the cars going to scrap, May 21, 1968. Richard E. Miller photo.

1-17. In 1960, a huge coal-fired electric generating plant opened in Bow, NH, and the B&M began moving coal to the plant in unit trains. Here, loaded Bow coal train LBA-48, drawn by mixed B&M and PennCentral/NYC power, is passing Gardner Tower on the long climb to East Gardner summit. At right, George C. Corey and his daughter Carol are taking in the action, May 24, 1968. Richard E. Miller photo.

1-18. As LBA-48 passes, a loud roaring sound in the west grows louder and louder, telling us there is a pusher on the end of the train. And here it is—it's B&M GP9 1728 giving it all she's got. The sound of roaring GP9s was common in the day and could be heard for miles around. Gardner, May 24, 1968. Richard E. Miller photo.

1-19. Worcester to Mechanicville freight WM-1 was a difficult train to photograph at Gardner as it left Worcester in the evening and—except on the longer days of the year—darkness would fall before it reached Gardner. But on this day, photographer Richard E. Miller caught the train coming off the Worcester Branch, May 24, 1968.

1-20. Piggybacks in WM-1's consist! Gardner, May 24, 1968. Richard E. Miller photo.

1-21. The Bow coal trains would provide many years of interesting train watching. At times, as many as three loaded coal trains a week passed through Gardner. Here's another one, led by B&M GP9 1739 with trailing PennCentral/NYC F-units, Aug. 18, 1968. Richard E. Miller photo.

1-22. Dispatcher William F. "Bill" Perry working at the CTC machine in Gardner Tower, Dec. 1968. Sometimes railroading ran in a family's blood. Perry, his father and three brothers were all Fitchburg Div. telegraph operators. On the CTC board, switches and color light signals could be set up for train movements with just the flick of a finger. The CTC machine at Gardner was retired on Jan. 23, 1969, when its functions were assumed by Greenfield. The Signal Dept. used the building for storage before it was razed in 1979 to make room for a passenger platform for the MBTA/B&M restored passenger service to Gardner that began Jan. 18, 1980. Richard E. Anderson photo.

1-23. B&M SW1 1117 idles on the Heywood Branch at Gardner Tower on a snowless December day in 1968. The steel drum next to the tower was filled with kerosene that was used in switch lamps about the yard. By this date, however, the switch lamps had been replaced by reflectorized markers. Richard E. Anderson photo.

1-24. On the Bow coal trains it was common to see "run through" foreign power. B&M power, in turn, sometimes ran offline as far west as the mines in the Midwest. Here we see B&M GP9 1728, GP18 1751, and four PennCentral pool units passing Gardner, Dec. 1968. Richard E. Anderson.

1-25. A New York Central caboose and pusher B&M SW9 1229 bring up the rear of the same train. It was a long climb to East Gardner, and the railroad did not like to risk stalling a heavy train on the grade. Gardner, Dec. 1968. Richard E. Anderson photo.

1-26. We include this image as a nod to the Providence & Worcester Railroad (P&W), which, by connecting with the B&M in Gardner, squeaked into the Monadnock Region. In July 1986, a week-long railroad convention in Boston—*Minuteman '86*—offered six railroad excursions, including this one on the P&W. Due to an ongoing labor dispute on Guilford Rail System, the passenger special was prohibited from using B&M rails to reach the passenger platform in Gardner. As a result of this difficulty, P&W's regular Worcester–Gardner freight, drawn by GP38s 2010 and 2011, arrived at Gardner with a seven-car passenger train and GP38 2009 tied on its tail end. The passenger train was cut off before the Rte. 2 Bridge south of Gardner Yard at the makeshift boarding area shown (South Main St.) and convention goers, who had been bussed out from Boston, boarded the cars and departed on a day-long excursion: Gardner–Worcester–Providence–Groton, CT–Worcester, July 23, 1986. Larry Kemp photo.

1-27. Interesting: eastbound Guilford freights, side-by-side at Gardner, March 1988. Alfred S. Arnold photo; B. G. Blodget coll.

1-28. Guilford 363, 615, and a third unit on an eastbound freight at Gardner, June 1989. B. G. Blodget photo.

1-29. A major derailment occurred on March 3, 2009, when twelve cars in a loaded coal train piled-up in the big rock cut west of the Otter River Bridge (B72.55) in Baldwinville. Both the road's wreck response trains—one from East Deerfield with a 250-ton capacity crane, the other from Waterville, Maine with a 200-ton capacity crane—were dispatched to the scene to work the wreck from the west and east ends of the cut respectively. The ex-B&M wreck response trains are an anachronism in today's world. Nearly all the other railroads in the country long ago switched to using contractors that respond to wrecks with over-the-highway equipment. Here is the Waterville wrecker—BM 3365 MW—paused at Gardner, March 5, 2009. B. G. Blodget photo.

Baldwinville (MP B70.53)

1-30. Looking west on the main line at the B&A diamond at Baldwinville. Note the B&A's freight house at right, mostly hidden by the B&M's freight house, ca. 1930. Photogr. unknown; B. G. Blodget coll.

1-31. A man gazes at General Motor's Electro-Motive Division FT 103 demonstrator passing Baldwinville with eastbound freight in Sept. 1940. There were not a lot of railfans chasing and photographing trains in 1940, so we are fortunate that some unknown probably knew what was going on and was trackside to snap this image. The 103, "the diesel that would revolutionize American railroading," tested on the B&M Sept. 5–15, 1940. The road would later take delivery of its first FTs in Sept. 1943 and as more units subsequently arrived, the Fitchburg Main Line between Boston and Mechanicville, NY, was quickly dieselized. Photogr. unknown; Narragansett Hist. Soc.

1-32. In the twilight of her service life in the mid-1950s, streamline train 6000, running as Trains 59/52 *Minute Man* between Troy, NY, and Boston, MA, seems to have been seldom photographed by railfans, intent at the time on documenting the last years of steam operations. Luckily, George H. Hill, B&M's official photographer, captured this image of Train 52 about to pass Baldwinville on a cold Jan. 15, 1954. The train had departed Athol at 9:33 a.m., made no stops before calling Gardner at 9:57, and would pull into North Station, Boston at 11:15. That "V" on the 6000's nose is a snow deflector that was attached during the winter months to improve visibility. The Baldwinville station buildings and the B&A diamond are behind Hill. Looking west, that is the Bridge St. Bridge, the Rte. 202 Bridge (beyond), and the Temple-Stuart Co. water tank at right. The switches are all shoveled clear and well brushed out. That essential piece of equipment for keeping the switches operational—a broom—hangs on a pole, far enough away from the tracks to keep it from being buried by a passing snowplow. Photo courtesy the B&MRRHS Archives.

1-33. GP9 1746 and two sister "Bluebirds," headed for Boston on piggyback train PB-2, pass furniture-maker Temple-Stuart's plant in Baldwinville, May 1, 1966. Richard E. Miller photo.

1-34. Back in PB-2's consist are new dump trailers waybilled for Boston Sand and Gravel, Baldwinville, May 1, 1966. Richard E. Miller photo.

1-35. Another loaded Bow-bound coal train, led by GP9 1736, west of Baldwinville, Sept. 7, 1967. Richard E. Miller photo.

1-36. An eastward through freight passes East Deerfield–to–Fitchburg train EF-2, waiting in the clear on the "dead track" at Baldwinville, March 1968. The "dead track" was a section of the old eastbound that had been left for switching purposes when the road from Parker (MP B66.51) to Wrights (MP B77.65) was single-tracked in 1961. Richard E. Miller photo.

1-37. In this view from the Bridge St. Bridge in Baldwinville, B&M SW9 1229 is pushing an eastbound freight. Notice the Baldwinville station and freight house are gone, Aug. 1971. Larry Kemp photo.

The Otter and Millers River Valleys

The western slope of the Monadnock Plateau between Gardner and Athol has always presented the road with the problem of getting along with the Otter and Millers Rivers, both known for their episodic, sometimes devastating rampages. The V&M chose an alignment with favorable graduation that followed these two rivers' valleys. In the day, there was a great rush to build railroads and this alignment was probably the quickest and cheapest to build. One section of this alignment of particular interest in our treatment area passed through southern Winchendon and Royalston, making a sweeping arc north of Birch Hill, crossing the Millers River, and continuing west on the north side of the river to Royalston. This section would undergo two major re-alignments in the ensuing years.

The first realignment happened in 1881–1882, when the Fitchburg—no doubt to address diabolical flooding issues—moved about five miles of the road in this area out of flood-prone swampland to higher ground (*Fitchburg Railroad Annual Rept.* 1882:12). The new alignment left the original V&M just west of the New Boston Road Crossing (X853 on the accompanying map), made a less dramatic arc westward, crossed the Otter River, and continued to Royalston on the *south* side of the Millers River.

At the time, nobody could possibly have foreseen the unimaginably devastating floods that lay ahead in 1936 and 1938. Iron girder bridge B76.20 west of Royalston was a casualty in the 1936 flooding. In the 1938 Hurricane, the Otter and Millers Rivers hit the B&M's Fitchburg Division between Gardner and Millers Falls with especial ferocity, leaving washouts and bridge outages in many places. The river took out the big two-track, rock-ballasted Otter River Bridge (B69.15) in Otter River.

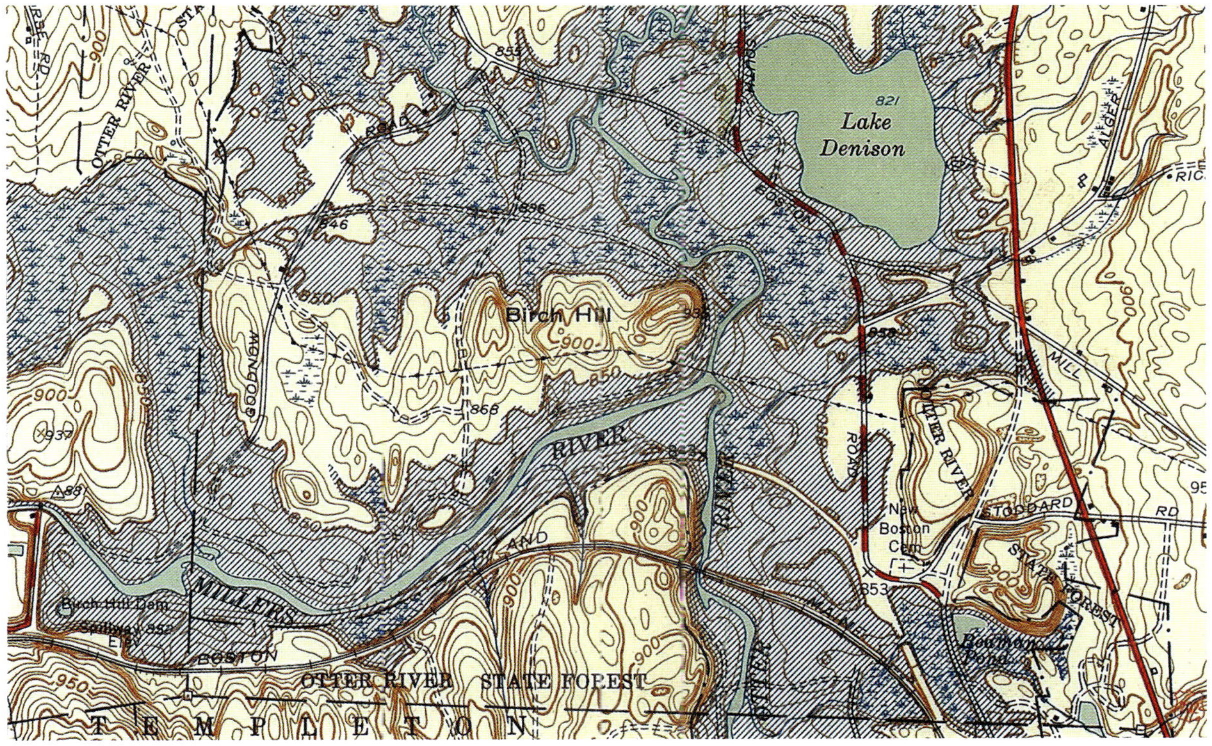

1-38. USGS topographic map (1954) showing, from top to bottom, the original 1847–1849 V&M alignment, and the 1881–1882 Fitchburg and 1940–1941 B&M/COE realignments in the Millers River Valley in southern Winchendon and Royalston. Each realignment was higher and further south than its predecessor. The slanted lines denote land subject to inundation following construction of the Birch Hill Flood Control Dam. Notice that the eastern end of the B&M/COE alignment unavoidably crosses part of this area—on a very high, heavily-armored embankment. Elevation point 853 marks the exact location of New Boston Crossing, a notoriously dangerous oblique crossing just west of New Boston Cemetery. The crossing was eliminated when New Boston Rd. was discontinued south of this point in 1940.

1-39. A B&M bridge crew has begun work to replace the Otter River Bridge (B69.15). The river's rampage left behind only this gaping washout—280 feet long and 40–50 feet deep—where the bridge had been. The bridge's forty-ton girder was later found, buried four feet deep in sand, Otter River, Sept. 1938. Photogr. unknown; B&MRRHS Archives.

CUTOVER EXERCISES AT SITE
9.30 A.M. E.S.T.

LUNCHEON - TOYTOWN TAVERN
WINCHENDON, MASS.
12.00 NOON - E.S.T.

HOST - BOSTON AND MAINE RAILROAD
MR. E.S. FRENCH - PRESIDENT

1-40. Cutover Exercises, west of Balwinville, July 22, 1941.

In 1939, the US Army Engineers (COE) entered the picture and, in 1940, the Birch Hill Dam Flood Control Project (as well as other allied projects in the Connecticut Valley) got underway. A vast area in Winchendon, Templeton, Phillipston, and Royalston was depopulated to create a dry basin to retain future flood waters. When filled to capacity, the basin flow line would reach the 850-foot contour. This meant that 4.5 miles of the Fitchburg Main Line between Baldwinville and Royalston—which over the years had become a modern double-track, signalized main line—would be in the basin, necessitating a second realignment.

B&M and Army Engineers began work October 7, 1940, even as the ominous clouds of World War II were gathering. The million dollar cost of moving the railroad, borne by the federal government, involved blasting a 2,600-foot cut as deep as forty feet through solid granite, building high fills, construction of a three-span 210-foot bridge over the Otter River west of Baldwinville in the town of Winchendon (note: this is a different Otter River Bridge than the one replaced at Otter River proper in 1938), and installation of new double-main, signalized track. The new B&M/COE track alignment, which shortened the distance between Baldwinville and Royalston by 0.23 miles (*B&M ETT* Nos. 31 and 32) was released for traffic on July 22, 1941, and the rails on the Fitchburg alignment were immediately pulled up by the Army Engineers.

1-41. All too typical hurricane damage, looking west from a point about a quarter mile east of Royalston. Visible in the distance is the Royalston freight house, miraculously spared by the storm, Sept. 1938. Photogr. unknown; B&MRRHS Archives.

1-42. Spike-driving ceremony marking the completion of the Birch Hill Dam Project's million dollar 4.5-mile main line track relocation between Baldwinville and Royalston and the opening of the new line. Officials and invited guests look on with interest as B&M president Edward S. French holds a silver spike and Army Engineers Lt. Col. Harvey Latson takes careful aim with the spike hammer. Notice the heavy rail! July 22, 1941. Robert J. Keller photo; B. G. Blodget coll.

1-43. Minutes following the dedication ceremony, Troy, NY–to–Boston Train 54, drawn by Pacific 3715, became the first regularly scheduled train to pass over the new track. Shown here entering the deep rock cut, 54 whistles past the special observation train that was pushed up from Royalston, bringing officials and guests out to the event. For sure, the conductor and engineer on 54 must have had orders to be "on the advertised" that day, July 22, 1941. Robert J. Keller photo; B&MRRHS Archives.

1-44. An eastbound freight, drawn by the 1737 and three sister GP9s, has just come through the rock cut and is stepping onto the 210-foot, rock-ballasted Otter River Bridge (B72.55), west of Baldwinville, ca. 1968. Richard E. Miller photo.

1-45. Still resplendent in her McGinnis "Bluebird" livery, westbound GP9 1749 leads three sisters into the big rock cut west of the Otter River Bridge (B72.55), late Spring 1976. Walter S. Kowal photo; Richard F. Kowal coll.

Great Times, Great Days—Railfanning west of Baldwinville

It was late spring of 1976—early June most likely—on a Saturday that my father Walter, Ron High, and myself got a call from old friend Phil O'Malley about two westbounds in the works. Information was harder to come by in those days—unless you had a scanner, which was expensive and changing channels with "crystals" was a tedious task. We took the drive from Worcester and the mile plus walk along the right-of-way to get into position. We waited almost three hours and got four westbounds! Symbol freights of the day were NE-87, LM-1, and RM-1 (or -3). I believe the accompanying photo was of NE-87, the freight that made a bridge connection with the Erie-Lackawanna. The early afternoon light was perfect and it was quite a show that day. The 1749 "Bluebird" on the lead really put the icing on the cake. Not too long after this photo was taken, the growth changed the site forever and made my father's image a rare one indeed.—*Richard F. Kowal*

1-46. The Beaman Brook Granite Arch, built by the V&M in the late 1840s—and viewable today—about 1,000 feet east of New Boston Crossing, on a section of the old V&M abandoned following the B&M/COE realignment in 1940–1941. May 14, 2022. Leo Landry photo.

Athol (MP B81.90)

1-47. While we regret the low resolution of this image, we judged it was just too interesting to leave behind. Fitchburg American (4-4-0) 31/*Marlboro* is stopped at the ornate Athol Union Station with an eastbound train. Engine 31 was built for the Fitchburg in 1867 by the McKay & Aldus Iron Works in East Boston. It went through several renumberings—the last to B&M 904 in 1900—and was scrapped at Keene in 1901 (Edson 1982). It is quite possible this image shows the opposite end of the same train pictured on page 46 in Volume I. The general deportment of people in the image—including that individual casually leaning on the engine—gives the impression the train is making a meal stop. In the day, the road owned no dining cars, and all meal stops were scheduled at Athol. The man standing next to the ball signal mast we would hazard is the ball tender, at the ready to perform his duties, Athol, ca. 1885–1891. Photogr. unknown. Photo courtesy Tom Pettee.

1-48. This is an eastward view of the B&A's three-stall roundhouse and small yard in Athol, ca. 1885–1891. The Fitchburg Main Line is outside the image to the left. The B&A also had a three-stall roundhouse— very similar to this one—at the end of its Ware River Branch in Winchendon (see page 172). George W. Moore photo. Photo courtesy Tom Pettee.

1-49. B&M's brand new Budd RDC-1 6100, the road's first Budd car, is open for showing at Athol, on its exhibition tour along "the Line of the Minute Man," April 22, 1952. Five days later, the car went into service on the Fitchburg Division between Boston and Troy, NY. George H. Hill photo; B&MRRHS Archives.

1-50. Pan Am leased (ex-CSX) six-axle units 7518 and 7517, trailed by GP40 319, still in Guilford livery, lead ED-9 at Athol, May 4, 2021. Pan Am Railways entered the history books on June 1, 2022, when it was purchased by CSX. Dale Monette photo.

CHAPTER TWO

THE CHESHIRE RAILROAD
The "Main Line of Cheshire County"

The Cheshire was built in 1843–1849. It was completed to Troy in December 1847, to Keene on May 16, 1848, and to a connection with the Sullivan Railroad in North Walpole on January 1, 1849. Freight and passenger service began January 8, 1849. In North Walpole, a temporary station was built—which it shared with the Sullivan—pending completion of both roads' bridges across the Connecticut River to Bellows Falls, Vermont. Passengers alighting from trains in North Walpole were conveyed across the Tucker Toll Bridge into Bellows Falls, Vermont, by stagecoach. In June 1849, the Cheshire's bridge at the Great Falls of the Connecticut—a covered, wooden, arched-truss bridge—was completed and rail service was extended the final 0.2 miles to the station in Bellows Falls proper. The Sullivan's bridge was completed in 1851.

The Cheshire, engineered to a gold standard and built to last a millennium, was widely hailed as one of the great engineering feats of its day. It was a single-iron road, its 53.75-mile main line stretching from South Ashburnham, Massachusetts, to Bellows Falls, Vermont. The road reached its highest elevation at 1,147 feet in Fitzwilliam, just west of Putnam (B78.34). The highest point between Keene and the Connecticut River was 830 feet at summit in the town of Surry. The four most remarkable features of the road included Gulf Bridge (B83.38) at Troy Ledges, the Joslin granite arch bridge (B89.41), Summit Cut in the town of Surry, and the bridge over the Great Falls of the Connecticut (B113.60) in North Walpole.

The Cheshire was always operated as a timetable east–west road. There were eight miles of passing sidings, 31.28 miles of tangent track, thirty-nine crossings at grade, and 1,939 feet of wooden bridges. Twenty granite arches were built along the road, including the Joslin Arch—a "daring" single-arch, keystone bridge over the East Branch of the Ashuelot River—the largest stone arch ever built in New Hampshire. There were extensive yard facilities and roundhouses at South Ashburnham, Keene, and North Walpole. The Cheshire and the Sullivan both had their own engine houses at North Walpole and a shared turntable. Section houses were located every four to six miles along the road.

In its early years, the road had wooden shops in Keene, which were replaced by brick, state-of-the-art shops in 1866. The following year, a fifteen-stall brick roundhouse was built adjacent to the shops. Eight American locomotives were home-built in the company shops (1868–1880). The conversion of locomotives from wood to coal burners was completed in 1888. The road changed out its original 60-pound iron rail to steel rail in 1876–1882.

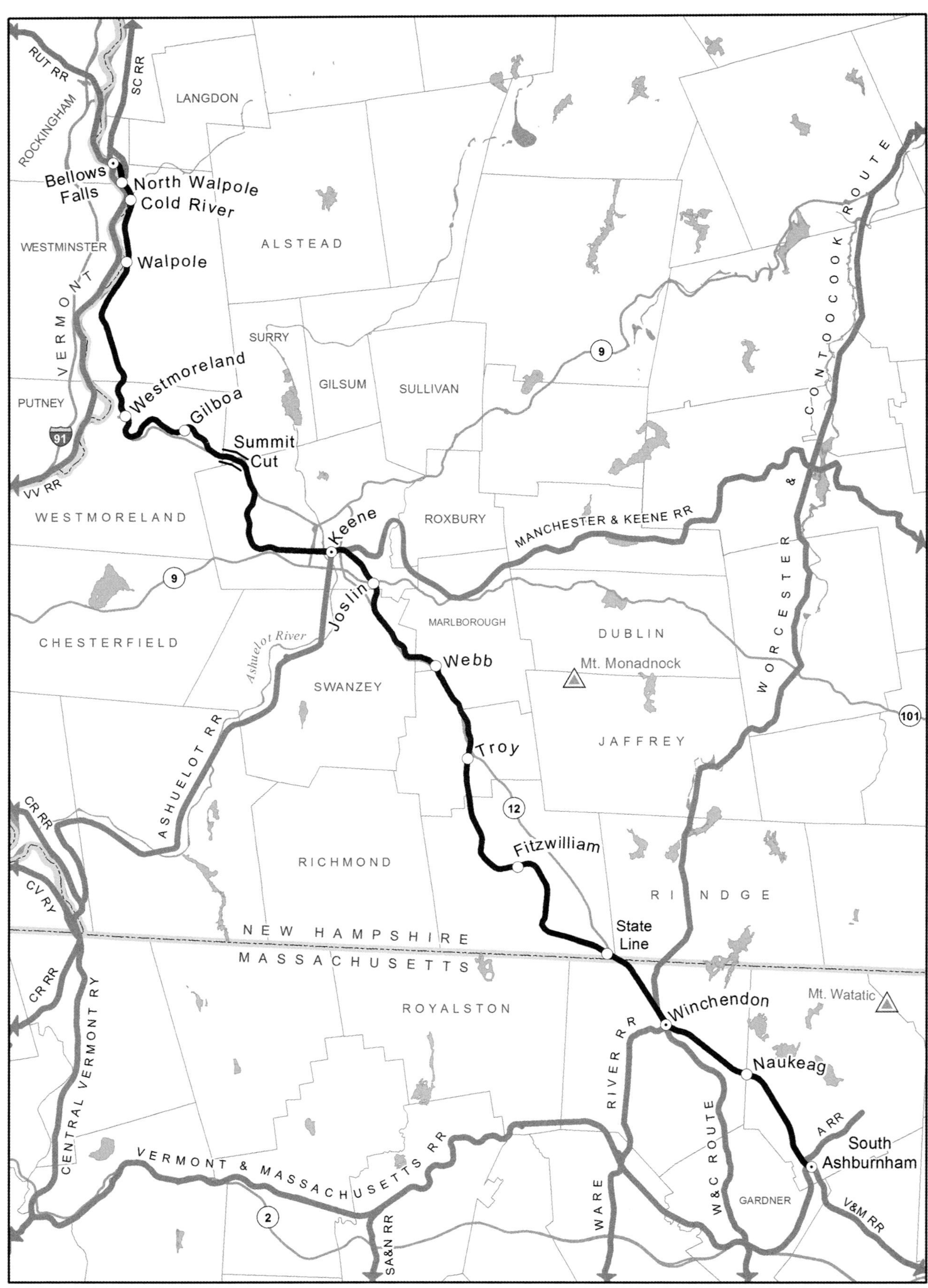

RUT RR
SC RR
ROCKINGHAM
LANGDON
Bellows
Falls
North Walpole
Cold River
WESTMINSTER
ALSTEAD
Walpole
VERMONT
9
Westmoreland
SURRY
GILSUM
SULLIVAN
PUTNEY
Gilboa
91
Summit
Cut
VV RR
WESTMORELAND
Keene
ROXBURY
MANCHESTER & KEENE RR
WORCESTER &
CONTOOCOOK ROUTE
9
Joslin
CHESTERFIELD
Ashuelot River
MARLBOROUGH
DUBLIN
Webb
Mt. Monadnock
SWANZEY
101
ASHUELOT RR
JAFFREY
Troy
CR RR
12
RICHMOND
Fitzwilliam
R I N D G E
CV RY
State
Line
NEW HAMPSHIRE
MASSACHUSETTS
ROYALSTON
Mt. Watatic
Winchendon
RIVER RR
Naukeag
CENTRAL VERMONT RY
CR RR
A RR
South
Ashburnham
VERMONT & MASSACHUSETTS RR
WARE
W & C ROUTE
GARDNER
V&M RR
2
SA&N RR

The Cheshire had direct connections with all the other roads in the Monadnock Region except for the Peterboro & Hillsboro (P&H). Overhead freight traffic on the Cheshire never approached the volume anticipated by its promoters, but over the years, indigenous industrial development sustained the road. In its forty-five years of independent operation, the Cheshire never pursued a policy of aggressive expansion. However, it temporarily operated the Ashuelot Railroad from 1860–1877, and in February 1879 assumed the lease of the Monadnock Railroad. The Cheshire was absorbed by the Fitchburg Railroad on October 1, 1890, and on July 1, 1900, the B&M leased the Fitchburg system. The Cheshire would continue on to the end as the B&M's "Cheshire Branch."

In its Fitchburg years, the Keene Shops became the road's largest repair facility and in 1899, the Fitchburg replaced the Cheshire's wooden covered bridge at the Great Falls of the Connecticut in North Walpole with a double-arch granite bridge (B113.60).

In the B&M years, a large menu of long-overdue improvements were made. Stations received orderboards in 1908–1809, block signals were installed in 1910–1911, the Keene Shops became the main locomotive facility for the road, and a new station was dedicated at Keene on January 24, 1911. Bridges were strengthened and mostly 100-pound rail installed in 1926–1929. The Cheshire remained a sand and gravel ballasted line. Engines grew heavier, but the heaviest allowed on the Cheshire Branch were Santa-Fe (2-10-2) and Pacific (4-6-2) types. The Santa Fe's were used on BX-1/XB-2, freight drags between Boston and Bellows Falls. These trains ran at night and hence were rarely, if ever, photographed on the Cheshire Branch.

Passenger service was remarkably good between the Monadnock Region and Boston. Streamline train 6000 ran as the *Cheshire* between White River Junction and Boston via Bellows Falls and Keene in 1944–1952. As a part of what the Fitchburg had once called "The Lake Champlain Route," the road handled two sets of named trains— the *Green Mountain Flyer* and the *Mount Royal*—between Boston and Montreal via its connection with the Rutland.

But alas, times were changing. Automobiles would kill the passenger business. One hundred and ten years of passenger service on the Cheshire ended with the final runs on May 31, 1958. Trucking competition after World War II and changing economic conditions led to a gradual erosion of freight traffic. It became a perfect storm of difficulties as the wayfreight business collapsed and long-time industries closed, burned down, or migrated to other parts of the country. Freight houses at most stations were closed in the 1950s. Overhead traffic interchanged at Bellows Falls dried up after the Rutland, hit by a strike in 1963, summarily shut down and went out of business. The profitable milk traffic handled from Bellows Falls to Boston ended in 1964 when the Bellows Falls Co-operative Creamery lost its milk contract with First National Stores. In its last years, traffic on the Cheshire Branch was reduced to occasional appearances of detouring trains, moves with over-dimension cars, and on-again, off-again locals operating out of Fitchburg when business warranted.

In 1961, the B&M sold Fitchburg Yard land and engine facilities in North Walpole to F. Nelson Blount for development as a museum for preservation and operation of steam locomotives. In the following two years, Blount's Monadnock, Steamtown and Northern Railroad reached an operating agreement with the B&M to run on the west end of the Cheshire Branch. Steam excursions were operated between Keene and Gilboa in 1962, and between North Walpole and Westmoreland in 1963.

In 1970, the B&M entered receivership, which only hastened the Cheshire Branch's demise. In 1972, the road between Winchendon and Swanzey (20.6 miles) and between Keene and Cold River (20.7 miles) was abandoned. Another 1.1 miles of track between Keene and Swanzey was given up in 1975. Remaining track at Keene was operated as the outer end of the Ashuelot Branch. The approximately ten miles of track left between South Ashburnham and Winchendon became a part of the Monadnock Branch. These last remaining segments were abandoned in 1984.

2-1. There is little doubt that this early photo—as well as the one on page 59 in Volume I—was commissioned by the Cheshire to commemorate a proud moment in the road's history. The occasion was the emergence of American 22/*Murdock* from the road's new, state-of-the-art locomotive shops. The 22/*Murdock*, shown here posed on the turntable at the roundhouse, was the first engine to be completely built in the home shops. The road would turn out seven more, the last in 1880. By then, the economics of scale had changed in favor of buying new locomotives directly from manufacturers. Quite likely, the two gentlemen in the picture are Ephraim Murdock Jr., Esq., the road's third president, honored by the naming of the engine, and master mechanic Frank A. Perry, who was credited with seeing through all the road's ambitious accomplishments. Looking down the tracks, the distant portals of the city's train shed station are visible. The wooden building across the tracks from the locomotive shops is one of the car shop buildings, Keene, 1868. J.W. Black photo; Benjamin Campbell and B. G. Blodget colls.

2-2. Keene Shops in Cheshire Railroad days, looking west, ca. 1885. A. A. Clough photo; Hist. Soc. Cheshire Cty.

2-3. By 1975, the eastern end of the Cheshire from South Ashburnham out to Winchendon had become, except for yard trackage in Keene, its last operating segment. After 1977, it had been included in the Monadnock Branch (South Ashburnham to Jaffrey), which the B&M received permission to abandon in 1984. In this westward view at the Rte. 12 bridge in North Ashburnham, rusty rails and the skeletal remains of an Automatic Block Signal tell of the branch's struggles in its last years. July 4, 1984. Leo Landry photo.

CHAPTER THREE

THE CHESHIRE RAILROAD: EAST END

South Ashburnham, Massachusetts (MP B59.90)

3-1. Three railroads—the V&M, the Cheshire, and the little Ashburnham—all met at South Ashburnham. Of course, at the time this image was shot—ca. 1935—all these lines were under the B&M flag. The track at the bottom is the Fitchburg Route Main Line and the Cheshire Branch curves across the image from the lower right to the upper left. The Ashburnham Branch, swinging off behind the big W. F. Whitney & Co. chair plant, was used in its last years for car storage until it was officially abandoned in 1937. It would appear that at least three Cheshire Branch tracks and two Ashburnham Branch tracks once crossed Pearl St. (Rte. 101) at grade. Nothing railroad in this aerial photo remains today, except for the Fitchburg Route Main Line—and it was single-tracked here in the early 1980s. Photogr. unknown; image courtesy of the Westminster Historical Society.

3-2. Looking west at the Rte. 101 crossing into the old Cheshire yard. The two curving tracks at right are the former Ashburnham Railroad tracks, abandoned at this time for more than a decade. South Ashburnham, June 3, 1949. Albert G. Hale photo; Walker Trans. Coll./Historic Beverly.

3-3. This is the less-frequently photographed eastward view at South Ashburnham, showing the station and small baggage room building. Across the tracks from the station is the W. F. Whitney Co. power plant, June 3, 1949. Albert G. Hale photo; Walker Trans. Coll./Historic Beverly.

Naukeag (North Ashburnham) (MP B64.03)

3-4. With nowhere to go, former B&M coach 1116 (late galley and dining car M3189 on the E. Deerfield wreck train) and caboose 104238 rest on a short piece of track aside Rte. 12 on the site where Naukeag station once stood. Everett L. Murray of Fitzwilliam, a retired street railway motorman, bought the two cars in 1963. The B&M delivered them to Winchendon and from there they were trucked to the site on a low-bed trailer. Lettered "Naukeag Shortline Railroad," they became a roadside curiosity. Murray and his wife Rose converted the M3189 into their home. Murray died in 1965, cutting short his plan to open the caboose as a small railroad museum. The coach eventually burned, but the caboose is still there, albeit barely recognizable what with a trailer-like home built over it. Naukeag, Aug. 1968. Richard E. Anderson photo.

3-5. FI-1, led by GP9R 1821, is westbound, approaching the Rte. 12 overhead bridge near Naukeag, Aug. 20, 1981. The FI-1 job, based in Fitchburg, ran out the length of what was then being called the Monadnock Branch—the cobbled together remaining segments of the Cheshire and Peterboro Branches—from South Ashburnham to the end of track just east of D. D. Bean in Jaffrey. It also made a side trip to Waterville when required. In later chapters, we will catch up with this train in Jaffrey and Waterville. Albert G. Hale photo; Walker Trans. Coll./Historic Beverly.

Winchendon (MP B67.92)

3-7. Winchendon station at a busy time. The right-hand track is the Peterboro Branch and the mile post at right shows the mileage from Worcester, ca. 1940. Photogr. unknown; B. G. Blodget coll.

3-8. Winchendon Station Agent James F. ("Jimmie") Farrell, always recognizable by his erect posture and impeccable attire, stands aloof at the far right with Freight Cashier Philip Cowick, ca. 1940. Farrell would retire from the B&M on Dec. 15, 1948, with fifty-six years in-point-of-service—sixteen of them as agent—at Winchendon. Photogr. unknown; B. G. Blodget coll.

3-9. Here comes the 6000, running as Train 5505 *Cheshire,* on its M-F late-afternoon trip over the Cheshire Branch to Bellows Falls and beyond to White River Jct. The train was almost always on time and people could set their clocks by it. The train is approaching Winchendon, has just crossed the B&A diamond, and will meet Train 5510 in the station at 4:29 p.m., July 1, 1947. Photogr. unknown; David S. Hutchinson coll.

3-10. Train 5508, the Montreal–Boston day train, drawn this day by E7 3819, has pulled in aside Train 8118 Mogul 1478, the Peterboro–Worcester local for their daily-except-Sunday afternoon meet at Winchendon. Usually 8118 would be in the station first and, if necessary, would wait fifteen minutes for 5508. Timetables show both trains departed Winchendon just after 2:00 p.m., the 5508 always first. Oct. 15, 1948. Albert G. Hale photo; Walker Trans. Coll./Historic Beverly.

3-11. Another meet of Trains 5508 and 8118, this day powered by big Pacific 3635 and a Mogul respectively, captured for posterity at Winchendon, ca. 1949. Alan Thomas photo; R. R. Conard and Benjamin Campbell colls.

3-12. Photographer Marium E. Foster, who was a correspondent for the *B&M Employee Magazine*, ti-tled this photo "The B&M Latest News." Sectionmen Augusto J. Santini and Arthur J. Courtemanche (holding their copies of the magazine) are on their motorcar at Winchendon, summer 1949. Hist. Soc. Cheshire Cty.

3-13. For a week-long test in Feb. 1951, the Budd Company's RDC-1 demonstrator 2960 operated between Boston and White River Jct. via Keene on the *Cheshire*'s time, making instrumented tests. It was rarely photographed on these runs, but here it is, caught making the inbound station stop at Winchendon. The photographer is standing on the station platform. The 2960 was the first Budd to run in revenue service anywhere on the B&M system. Its appearance presaged the retirement of the road's ancient fleet of wooden coaches. The B&M would eventually purchase 109 Budds from 1952 through 1958 and become the largest operator of these cars in the world. Marium E. Foster photo; Hist. Soc. Cheshire Cty.

3-14. It was May 30, 1958, the day before scheduled passenger trains would make their final runs over the Cheshire Branch, when B&M dispatcher Preston S. Johnson rode out to Bellows Falls, capturing images along the road from the cab window of an RDC. This shot, at the north end of the Winchendon yard, beautifully captures where the Cheshire and Peterboro Branches part company—the Cheshire heading straight ahead, the Peterboro swinging off to the right, passing the switch for the Davenport Coal trestle/shed. The two Jackson Ave. grade crossings (one for each branch), once protected by a single crossing tender, have only recently been equipped with flashers. The huge building once belonged to toymaker M. E. Converse Co. Converse closed in 1934 and the plant was purchased by furniture maker Sprague & Carlton Co. Photo by Preston S. Johnson; coll. of Wayne D. Hills.

Preston S. Johnson kept a journal detailing every day that he worked for the B&M from January 1, 1942 until he retired. He lived in Concord, New Hampshire between 1955 and April 1958, then moved to Melrose, Massachusetts. Johnson's journal entry for May 30, 1958, read: "Day off. Rode Talgo to Boston No. 605 unit 6101 to Fitchburg. Engine caught fire at Leominster. No. 651 to Bellows Falls. Had lunch and [rode] No. 78 to Springfield and B&A No. 424 to Boston and No. 151 to Melrose. Dick Schmidt met me at Fitchburg. Nice trip. Rode up front with Engineer Dan Russell." —*From the Journal of Preston S. Johnson, courtesy of Wayne D. Hills*

3-15. Looking outward at the Winchendon diamond, notice the switch ties remain where the Peterboro track once joined the B&A track. The Cheshire Branch crossed the Millers River on the high-sided bridge (the so-called "Black Bridge") at left. April 21, 1962. Albert G. Hale photo; Walker Trans. Coll./ Historic Beverly.

State Line (MP B70.93)

3-16. Tangent track west of State Line, Old Turnpike Road crossing in the distance, April 1913. Photogr. unknown; B. G. Blodget coll.

3-17. Train 5507 Pacific 3711, with at least four milk cars on the head pin, passing State Line under a lowering sky, April 7, 1951. Stanwood K. Bolton photo.

3-18. Traffic is stopped at the Rte. 12 crossing for Train 5507, now handled by just a single RDC-1, State Line, July 29, 1954. Albert G. Hale photo; Walker Trans. Coll./Historic Beverly.

Fitzwilliam (MP B76.28)

3-19. Fitzwilliam station in Cheshire days, when the railroad advertised the distance from Boston on all its stations, ca. 1885. Photogr. unknown; B. G. Blodget coll.

3-20. Fitzwilliam station, looking eastward at the Laurel Lake Road Crossing, ca. 1945. Albert G. Hale photo; Walker Trans. Coll./Historic Beverly.

Rockwood (MP B79.22)

3-21. Rockwood was a railroad location—its significance, a long, 64-car passing siding—about three miles west of Fitzwilliam at Rockwood Pond. It last appeared in ETT No. 14 dated April 30, 1933. This is it, looking west, Rockwood Pond at right, the crossing sign at Rockwood Pond Road visible in the distance, April 1913. Photogr. unknown; B. G. Blodget coll.

Troy (MP B81.55)

3-22. Consolidation 2702 at Troy station, June 3, 1939. Albert G. Hale photo; Walker Trans. Coll./Historic Beverly.

3-23. The railroad's Gulf Bridge (B83.88) accommodated both the South Branch of the Ashuelot River and the Keene Road. The two never got along very well together in "the Gulf," a deep gorge of the river at Troy Ledges, and they were separated in 1943–1945. The Keene Road was moved out of the Gulf to where it is today (Rte. 12). Another project came along in 1983, when a huge box culvert was installed beneath both the railroad's Gulf Bridge and the Rte. 12 Bridge—and then the whole area was filled. The area, as it once was, is completely unrecognizable today. In this image, Pacific 3656 is westbound on Train 5503 *Green Mountain Flyer* at Gulf Bridge/Troy Ledges before all of the changes, Troy, June 3, 1939. Albert G. Hale photo; Walker Trans. Coll./Historic Beverly.

Joslin (South Keene) (MP B89.22)

3-24. Mogul 1426, lifting a car from the Keene Chair factory, crosses Marlborough St. and the KERy. The engineer appears to have his hand on the whistle cord and is delivering a long blast as he moves over the crossing. The B&M crossed Marlborough St. (and the KERy) on three industrial tracks. The two closest tracks were used as a switchback to reach the Cole grist mill. Whistling for every crossing, there could be no mistaking when the train was in town. South Keene, ca. 1920. Photogr. unknown; Benjamin Campbell coll.

(*opposite page*) 3-23A. With both the Keene–Troy Road and the South Branch of the Ashuelot River side-by-side beneath the Gulf Bridge (B83.88), things could sometimes turn ugly. This image shows what the scene looked like this day to a driver heading to Troy. Note that the portion of the bridge over the river was open-deck, while the portion over the road was high-sided to protect traffic below, Troy, March 12, 1936. Photogr. unknown; Jim Dufour coll.

3-25. Pacific 3600, B&M's very first Pacific—one of twelve built for the road by Schenectady in 1910—crosses Joslin Arch with an eastbound train. The car sandwiched between two baggage cars that looks like an RPO/coach, is actually an RPO car (notice no vestibules). undated. Photogr. unknown; Benjamin Campbell coll.

3-26. Pacific 3622 with a train westbound on the Joslin Arch, ca. 1920. Photogr. unknown; Benjamin Campbell coll.

3-27. Running with a conventional consist, Train 5506 *Cheshire*, led by E7 3802, is at the Joslin Arch, eastbound for Boston, April 18, 1953. George C. Corey photo. (See Vol. I, p. 104 for Stanwood K. Bolton's rendition of the same train.)

WHEN THE *CHESHIRE* CARRIED AN RPO

Between November 1944 and late April 1952, B&M Train 5506 *Cheshire* operated White River Junction–Bellows Falls–Boston using the B&M's streamline train 6000. The Spring Time Table, effective April 27, 1952, included a number of changes that affected the *Cheshire*. B&M Train 5504 *Mount Royal* was dropped and the RPO it had handled between Bellows Falls and Boston was added to the *Cheshire's* consist. It was at this time the 6000 was taken off the *Cheshire*, reassigned to the *Minute Man* (operating between Boston and Troy, New York), and replaced by a conventional train. In George Corey's April 18, 1953, photo of Train 5506, notice the first car behind the locomotive is a B&M baggage-RPO (30-foot apartment) car from the B&M 3115–3121 series. This car actually operated from Montreal, Quebec, via the Rutland Railroad with a US Postal Service crew. The car changed trains at Rutland and continued on to Bellows Falls as Rutland Train 146 arriving at 2:20 a.m. (DST). The Bellows Falls Switcher added the B&M baggage-RPO car to our B&M Train 5506 *Cheshire* that departed Bellows Falls for Boston at 7:40 am (DST). Our B&M train also included a B&M or Maine Central wood-bodied, steel underframe, baggage-express car, shown following the RPO car. Not in view would normally have been a couple of B&M coaches, including a deluxe streamline (stainless steel) coach. This arrangement would be short lived, as the Rutland, crippled by a strike on June 26, 1953, shut down—and never restored—its passenger service. The Fall Time Table, effective September 27, 1953, shows the conventional train replaced by an RDC. —COL (Ret.) Tom E. Thompson

CHAPTER FOUR

THE CHESHIRE RAILROAD: KEENE

4-1. The J. P. Rust Pail Co., a maker of wooden pails, was a B&M customer with a siding off the Cheshire Branch in Keene. It later became Keene Woodenware. Its plant once sprawled over several acres east of Main St. At the far right in this image (see detail), notice the Cheshire Branch Main Line and the parallel Manchester & Keene (Keene Branch) to its right. The M&K rises on a steady one percent grade, necessary to gain sufficient elevation to swing over the Cheshire on the covered Eastern Avenue Bridge (visible in the distance), Keene, ca. 1905. Photogr. unknown; Hist. Soc. Cheshire Cty.

4-2. West of Island St., the Cheshire had a two-mile stretch of tangent track. This image shows part of the straightaway, looking west from Pearl St. The opposite whistle posts are halfway between Pearl and West Sts., Keene, April 1913. Photogr. unknown; B. G. Blodget coll.

4-3. Introducing the new *Flying Yankee*, B&M advertisement, 1935. This was big—really big, especially coming as it did in the depths of the Great Depression.

4-4. Brand-new streamline train 6000 is open for inspection at Keene, as hundreds of people are queued up for a chance to go through the train, March 22, 1935. This would be the last time they would see the train until Nov. 1, 1944, when it began running as the *Cheshire*. Photogr. unknown.

4-5. Streamline train 6000, running as Train 5506 *Cheshire*, at Eastern Ave., Keene, Sept. 23, 1948. Albert G. Hale photo; Walker Trans. Coll./Historic Beverly.

The Keene Switcher

The Keene Switcher was an interesting job. It was always a one-trick operation. At 8:00 a.m., the hostler would bring the engine up from the engine house to the station, where the crew signed in, received orders, and began their day. To minimize the number of Main Street crossings, the west yard was worked in the morning, the east yard in the afternoon. The job's working limits were the Keene Yard Limits.

The Keene Switcher's duties included spotting, shifting, and lifting cars on consignees' sidings, as well as less-than-carload cars at the freight house. Cars brought up from East Deerfield on EK-1, as well as cars dropped by WX-1/XW-2 would be spotted on consignees' sidings. The switcher would make up KE-2's train and set off any cars for pickup by WX-1/XW-2. In the 1950s and 1960s, there were always 25–30 steady rail customers. Even as late as 1981, there were still a dozen industries in Keene using rail.

From the late 1940s through the early 1960s, the assigned power for the Keene Switcher was usually a GE 44-tonner. The B&M had purchased ten of these units (110–119) in 1940–1948. The job called for a four-man crew—a conductor, an engineer, and two brakemen. Under an agreement with the Brotherhood of Locomotive Engineers, no fireman was required on engines under 45 tons working within Yard Limits. In rare instances when the job was required to go out on the road to Joslin or Webb, a fireman had to be called, even if it meant taxiing a fireman out from East Deerfield. The 44-tonners were also used at times in the yards at Gardner and Bellows Falls, where the same rules applied.

By the late 1960s, as freight cars were becoming larger and heavier, the 44-tonners were superseded by more powerful EMD (usually SW1s) and Alco switchers. When a unit came due for maintenance, it would be swapped out for a "fresh" engine. The replacement engine and the one it replaced would typically move on a road job such as WX-1/XW-2. Here are several pictures of the 44-tonners at work in Keene.

4-6. During peak travel periods for holidays, camp traffic, and the summer trade, the Keene Switcher was called upon for another duty. In the day, people traveling somewhere to stay any length of time would bring along huge wooden trunks. During busy times, traffic in and out of Keene could be of such volume that a baggage car would sometimes be attached to the end of passenger trains. The Keene Switcher would wait in the clear for a train to arrive in the station and then would rush out to pull the baggage car off or tie one onto the end as required (V. M. Zolinsky, personal recollections). Here we see the 115 attending to this duty on the end of an eastbound train. Keene, May 21, 1949. Stanwood K. Bolton photo.

4-7. GE 44-tonner 110 eases out of the yard and across Main St. with a cut of cars. Keene, summer 1957. Photogr. unknown; David S. Hutchinson coll.

4-8. Working the Keene Switcher job, the 118 pauses in front of the C. A. Jones Building on Railroad St., May 1961. Alan Thomas photo; William A. Gleason coll.

4-9. In the weeks following the Great Hurricane of Sept. 21, 1938, the main line between East Deerfield and Gardner was out of service due to track damage in the Millers River Valley (see Chapter 1). During this period, the Cheshire Branch, which suffered less severe damage, played a critical route for detouring trains. Photographer Albert G. Hale caught what is probably one of them—an eastbound double-header, led by Consolidation 2701, approaching the Marlborough St. Bridge, Keene, Oct. 15, 1938. Walker Trans. Coll./Historic Beverly.

4-10. XW-2, Keene, Sept. 5, 1950. Albert G. Hale photo; Walker Trans. Coll./Historic Beverly.

4-11. B&M Train 654, RDC-1 6100, the last scheduled eastbound passenger train on the Cheshire Branch, making a station stop at Keene, Saturday May 31, 1958, with photographer Alan E. MacMillan Sr. and sons Alan Jr. and David onboard. Photo courtesy Alan E. MacMillan Jr.

4-12. Alco RS3 1542 resting east of Main St., Keene, July 1, 1960. Alan Thomas photo; William A. Gleason coll.

4-13. The Keene section house, looking a bit weather-beaten, July 14, 1962, Richard E. Anderson photo.

4-14. The roundhouse and turntable, Sept. 15, 1962. Albert G. Hale photo; Walker Trans. Coll./Historic Beverly.

4-15. At Keene, Monadnock, Steamtown & Northern 15 is all ready to depart on another trip to Gilboa, Sept. 1962. J. Brennan Lowell photo; Walker Trans. Coll./Historic Beverly.

4-16. The B&M's bicentennial engine 200 and exhibit car open on the old freight house siding east of Main St., Keene, July 15, 1976. Larry Kemp photo.

4-17. There being no trains to Keene in over a year, the sounds of diesel horns were again heard in the Ashuelot Valley in May 1984. It was the B&M running out to Keene (from Brattleboro) with gondolas for lifted rail. Here are three of the cars, spotted at the west end of the yard, waiting to be loaded. The curved track at left center is the west leg of the wye. The photographer is standing at the west end of the roundhouse, looking west. Note, in order westward, the low girder bridge over the old Colony Mill power canal, the Island St. crossing, and the steel truss Ashuelot River Bridge beyond. Keene, May 11, 1984. Leo Landry photo.

CHAPTER FIVE

THE CHESHIRE RAILROAD: WEST END

Walpole (MP B109.82)

5-1. The freight agency at Walpole was closed and the station was retired in 1960. The agent's duties were transferred to Bellows Falls and Walpole became a carload-only station. Bridge Fuel and Grain would continue as a railroad customer until the line was abandoned. Looking westward at the now boarded-up station, April 21, 1962. Albert G. Hale photo; Walker Trans. Coll./Historic Beverly.

Cold River (MP B112.57)

5-2. Here is the rarely photographed street (Rte. 12) side of the Cold River combination flag station and freight house. In the foreground is the Cold River Spur, which at times also served as a team track (see Vol. I, p. 133). The main line is on the other side of the building. Undated. Benjamin Campbell coll.

5-3. Train 5503 *Green Mountain*, Pacific 3656, Cold River, Oct. 12, 1938. Albert G. Hale photo; Walker Trans. Coll./Historic Beverly.

5-4. Ex-B&M RDC-1 6154 with ex-NYC RDC-1 M453 keeping company behind, await better days at end of track, Cold River, May 15, 2021. Frederick G. Bailey photo.

North Walpole (MP B113.50) and Fitchburg Yard

5-5. Train 5503 *Green Mountain*, E7 3809, on the Granite Arch Bridge, North Walpole, April 30, 1950. Bernice B. Perry photo; Milford Historical Society.

5-6. At the time this shot was taken, the old Fitchburg Yard and roundhouse in N. Walpole, sold by the B&M to F. Nelson Blount in 1961, were still owned by the Blount estate's Green Mountain Railroad. The B&M, however, had retained ownership of its main line (left) between Cold River and the New Hampshire state line (including the granite arch bridge) and the use of a layover track in the yard. GP7 1563 has most likely brought FX-1 out from Fitchburg and is laying over before returning to Fitchburg. N. Walpole, Feb. 1968. Richard E. Anderson photo.

5-6A. The Green Mountain Railroad (GMRC) hosted an open house at its engine facilities in the old Fitchburg Yard for the Rutland Railroad Historical Society's 1992 annual meeting, being held that year in Bellows Falls. In the 1980s, the GMRC, in need of more power, had taken advantage of a flood of GP9s coming on the market, as big railroads rushed to upgrade their fleets with new generation locomotives. Posed, left to right, at the engine house are the four GP9s the GMRC had acquired: 1849 (ex-Burlington Northern), 1851 (ex-Norfolk Southern), 1850 (ex-Chesapeake & Ohio), and 1848 (ex-Bangor & Aroostook), North Walpole, NH. May 16, 1992. Richard E. Anderson photo.

Bellows Falls, VT (MP B113.83) and Rutland Yard

5-7. This is a northward view along the B&M's Connecticut River Main Line, shot from the Bellows Falls station platform. Trains departing northward would cross the Rutland diamonds and the steel truss bridge across the Connecticut River. The Rutland's Main Line (used by Cheshire Branch trains to reach the station), crosses the picture left to right. That is the ball signal and its tender's shanty at right center. The ball signal controlled the diamond crossing; In this image, the signal is set (three balls) for the B&M Main Line. Tracks curving to the left are the connecting tracks to the Rutland Railroad. The Rutland owned most of the railroad infrastructure on the Bellows Falls "Island," including its steel truss canal bridge (left), roundhouse, and water tank (right). The sweeping Bellows Falls Arch Bridge, visible in the background, was a highway/pedestrian bridge. When built in 1905, it was the largest arch bridge in the United States. Bellows Falls, undated. Albert G. Hale photo; Walker Trans. Coll./ Historic Beverly.

5-8. A southbound train approaches the Bellows Falls station, Aug. 21, 1940. Paul M. Pearson photo; B&MRRHS Archives.

5-9. Rutland 92 was one of four Mountains (4-8-2s, 90–93) the road purchased from Alco in Sept. 1946. A picture of this engine, taken in Fitchburg Yard, North Walpole, NH, by Dwight A. Smith on June 10, 1950, appeared on page 142 in Volume I. Here is another image of the same engine in steam in Rutland Yard, Bellows Falls, ca. 1951. The lives of the Mountains were cut short by dieselization; all four were already out of service by the end of 1952. Roads at the time were not in the market for new steam power and when no buyers appeared, they were scrapped in March 1955. V. M. Zolinsky photo.

5-10. B&M Passenger Extra RDC-2 6212, ready to depart Bellows Falls, VT, for Fitchburg, MA, with a Dept. of Public Utilities inspection train. Note white flag on the far end of car. Aug. 1963. Alan E. Mac-Millan Sr. photo; Collection of his son, Alan Jr.

5-11. Springfield-to-White River Jct. SJ-1 Extra 4266 north is crossing Depot St., Bellows Falls. Colored-light CTC signals have replaced the old ball signal system here and the ball tender's shanty stands unused. The curving tracks connect to the Green Mountain Railroad (the former Rutland). May 30, 1966. Richard E. Miller photo.

5-12. Springfield-to-White River Jct. Train 75 *Ambassador* has just cleared the Rutland diamonds and the photographer has captured the Bellows Falls station and freight house from the rear of the train. Weeds rule the former Rutland Yard. July 1, 1966. Richard E. Miller photo.

CHAPTER SIX

THE CHESHIRE RAILROAD: WRECKS AND MISADVENTURES

It seems the Cheshire suffered a spate of fairly serious accidents in the late-1870s—and we have learned of yet another one. At about 1:00 a.m., April 1, 1878, some 1.5 miles above (west of) Westminster station on the Fitchburg's V&M Division, a wheel broke on the third car from the engine on a fourteen-car stock train. It and all eleven following cars derailed. Eight cars were pitched down a steep embankment and were all smashed up. A wreck train left Fitchburg for the scene of the accident about 3:30 a.m. According to the *Fitchburg Sentinel*, "The work of clearing the track was pushed so vigorously that the morning express train from North Adams was delayed less than fifteen minutes." There were 803 hogs and an unspecified number of sheep on the train. Two hundred and fifty hogs, either killed in the accident or slaughtered, were loaded onto flatcars and forwarded to Cambridge to be rendered into lard oil.

Before the coming of Automatic Block Signals in 1909, the number of wrecks on the Cheshire was awful. Unlike other single-iron roads in the Monadnock Region, the Cheshire—with heavier traffic, faster speeds, and visibility issues in some areas due to curves and rock cuts—was a particularly dangerous road. Crewmen kissed their wives and families good-bye every day they went to work, not knowing whether they would return.

6-2. During the Great Hurricane of Sept. 21, 1938, Train 5511 *Mount Royal* came to grief about 1.5 miles west of Naukeag after it ran upon a section of track washed out along the flooding Millers River. Derailed cars were picked up and the track reopened fairly quickly, but the train's power, Pacific 3621, down the embankment and well dug into a marshy area, lay beside the track for over a month before she was rescued. The railroad had far worse problems to deal with first. Winchendon, Oct. 15, 1938. Albert G. Hale photo; Walker Trans. Coll./Historic Beverly.

(*opposite page*) 6-1. Here we see Fitchburg westbound Train 24, Ten-Wheeler 233 (ex-Cheshire 33), in trouble at Westmoreland, May 28, 1891. It had rear-ended another westbound—a "wild train" (extra)— that had stopped for orders at Westmoreland station. Train 24's conductor had been cautioned to look out for the train ahead, but the engineer had rounded a curve so fast that a quick stop was impossible (*Sentinel* May 28, 1891). The railroad workers are on the scene—and the slow film reveals who is really working and who isn't! Photogr. unknown; Hist. Soc. Cheshire Cty.

6-3. Keene residents awoke Sunday morning, March 22, 1959, to learn that in the early morning hours, Train 650, the eastbound milk train, had encountered an open switch and derailed in the East Yard. Lead unit GP7 1576, trailing unit F2 4260, and the lead milk car left the iron. After about a two-hour delay, the remaining eleven milk cars on the train were cut off and forwarded to Boston. A wreck train from East Deerfield arrived in the afternoon (*Sentinel* March 23, 1959). In this image, we see the wreck train has been backed into the East Yard and the wreck crane cut off. The milk car has already been rerailed and moved out of the way. As an aside, notice the kerosene switch lamp; kerosene lamps remained in use here into the mid-1960s. Photogr. unknown; Rick Kfoury coll.

6-4. Now we see SW9 1224, probably the wreck train's power, has moved the "big hook" into position and is lifting the 4260 back on the iron. According to the *Sentinel*, "the last engine left under its own power about 8 o'clock." Keene, March 22, 1959. Photogr. unknown; Rick Kfoury coll.

CHAPTER SEVEN

THE CHESHIRE RAILROAD:
SPECIAL, LATE, AND LAST MOVES

Symbol freights FX-1/XF-2 between Fitchburg and Bellows Falls, which had been annulled in June 1961, were restored in the fall of 1967 and ran off-and-on as needed for about a year. The job would run out to Bellows Falls, lay over in North Walpole, and return east the following day. It performed all local work both ways except at Keene, where the Keene Switcher would handle drops and assemble pickups. We followed XF-2 with H. Bentley Crouch on June 20, 1968 (see Volume I, page 167). Now, in the following seven images, we accompany Richard E. Anderson as he chased another XF-2 from Bellows Falls as far as Keene on a beautiful day in October 1968.

7-1. Quite likely the Bellows Falls Switcher has assembled the train for XF-2 in the old Rutland Yard and GP7 1573 has come over from N. Walpole to pick up the train. We'll soon be on the way.

7-2. Crossing the granite arch bridge (B113.60), N. Walpole.

7-3. On the Cold River iron truss bridge, N. Walpole.

7-4. Entering London Cut, Westmoreland.

7-5. On the granite arch bridge (B94.57) on Chesterfield Rd., W. Keene. This arch is still intact today.

7-6. Though few people knew the word "decarbonization" in the late 1960s, use of coal was already in long-term decline for various reasons. Yet, B&M was still handling carload coal for many small New England dealers. Here, XF-2 passes a coal hopper spotted at the Chabot Coal tipple, West Yard, Keene.

7-7. It appears there has been some combination of drops and pickups in the West Yard as the first five cars (at least) in the consist have changed. The yellow car is a Fruit Growers Express refer—interesting. Its work in Keene completed, XF-2 heads off through the East Yards, passing the Keene Switcher SW1 1115.

7-8. F7 4265 leads a vat train crossing the iron truss bridge at Cold River, Jan. 4, 1969. Donald S. Robinson photo; Walker Trans. Coll./Historic Beverly.

7-9. The afternoon shadows have lengthened as 4265 approaches the Central St. crossing in Winchendon with the same train. The Beef Shop stands where the station once stood, Jan. 4, 1969. Richard E. Miller photo.

7-10. GP7 1564 leads another vat train moving over the Mountain Track to Fitchburg Yard, North Walpole, Feb. 16, 1969. Donald S. Robinson photo; Walker Trans. Coll./Historic Beverly.

7-11. GP9 1706 westbound at Fitzwilliam with an over-dimension move, undated. Donald S. Robinson photo; Walker Trans. Coll./Historic Beverly.

CHAPTER EIGHT

THE ASHUELOT RAILROAD
The Valley Route to Keene

Chartered December 27, 1844, the Ashuelot Railroad—backed by the Connecticut River Railroad (CRRR)—was built up its namesake river valley between East Northfield, Massachusetts, and Keene in 1849–1851. It was the second road to reach Keene and would be the last to be abandoned there. The road's most striking structure was its large bridge across the Connecticut River—a reverse truss, open deck, wooden bridge between South Vernon, Vermont and Hinsdale (the "East Northfield Bridge"). The road closely followed the Ashuelot River to Keene, crossing the river four times on wooden truss bridges. All these bridges were later ironized. The Ashuelot was a 24-mile, single-iron, unsignalized road with 1.57 miles of passing sidings. The original track was 58-pound rail—upgraded to mostly 100-pound rail by 1930—laid on gravel ballast. There were about eight miles of curved track, sixteen miles of tangent track. The average grade was 0.34 percent, the ruling grade 0.65 percent between Hinsdale and Ashuelot. There were nineteen crossings at grade.

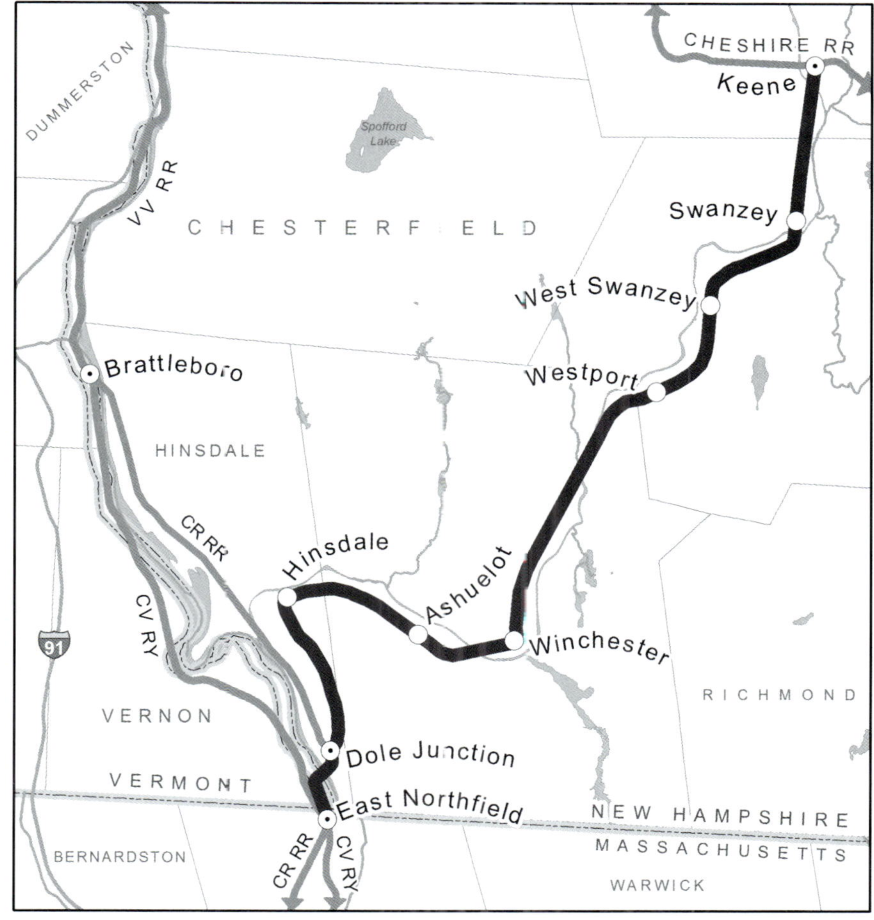

In its independent years, the Ashuelot leased itself to other roads for its operation. It was initially leased to the CRRR from January 1851 through 1860, then to the Cheshire from January 1861 to April 20, 1877, and then to the CRRR again until February 6, 1890. The road was furnished by its lessees. On February 7, 1890, the Ashuelot was merged into the CRRR, which was in turn leased by the B&M in 1893.

The Ashuelot River below Keene was an industrial mecca. Water-powered mills and coal-fired steam mills flourished in the valley, turning out paper, wooden boxes, furniture, and other woodenware. The Ashuelot prospered along with its online industry. It also had some importance as part of a detour route when there was trouble on the Fitchburg or Connecticut River Main Lines.

In 1912–1913, a new section of the Connecticut River Main Line connecting East Northfield and Brattleboro was built through western Hinsdale. This project appropriated the first two miles of the Ashuelot—including the East Northfield Bridge (S50.52)—up to a point that became known as Dole Junction. Operations continued

uneventfully until June 1970, when the East Northfield Bridge developed problems and was taken out of service. Subsequently, Ashuelot Branch trains would reach Dole Junction from Brattleboro via what came to be known as the Fort Hill Branch (see Chapter 14).

From the early 1930s until a last run on January 5, 1952, a gas-electric motorcar or "doodlebug" handled the passenger service between East Northfield and Keene. Freight service was handled by locals from East Deerfield or Brattleboro. Throughout the 1970s and early 1980s, the B&M was struggling in bankruptcy and looking to reduce costs. It leased the operation of the Keene Yard to the Green Mountain Railroad effective January 23, 1978, and on January 1, 1982, transferred operations on the Fort Hill Branch and the entire Ashuelot Branch to the Green Mountain, cutting back interchange with the Green Mountain to Brattleboro. However, due to the Ashuelot Branch's advanced stage of disrepair, all service ceased after November 1, 1983, and the B&M abandoned the line and all remaining trackage in Keene. In May 1984, the B&M operated several salvage trains to Keene to drop off gondolas for the retrieval of lifted rail.

South Vernon, Vermont/East Northfield, Massachusetts (MP S49.67)

8-1. Looking north at the new South Vernon, VT, station . . . in West Northfield, MA, 1910. The bridge carries East Northfield Rd. across the tracks—B&M at left, CV at right. The name of this station was changed to East Northfield in 1915. Confused? Read about East Northfield in Volume I, pages 206–207. Postcard; Scott J. Whitney coll.

Dole Junction (MP S51.90)

8-2. The conductor has signed the train off the Ashuelot Branch and Keene to East Deerfield KE-2, Consolidation 2424, is pulling onto the main line at Dole Jct., Nov. 11, 1937. Albert G. Hale photo; Walker Trans. Coll./Historic Beverly.

8-3. The RRE's *Rural New England Excursion* covered parts of several Fitchburg Division branches. The train consisted of Mogul 1415, Atlantic 3235, ten coaches, and a diner. Here, the special has come down the Ashuelot Branch from Keene and is waiting at Dole Jct. for permission to enter the main line. Note the main line's bridge over Rte. 63 at left. Last steam on the Ashuelot, June 10, 1951. Donald S. Robinson photo; Walker Trans. Coll./Historic Beverly.

8-4. Drawn this day by Alco S4 1274, KE-2 is arriving at Dole Jct. with a very typical consist. The conductor will call the Greenfield dispatcher for permission to enter the main line. Other than the GP9s, the 1274 was the only B&M engine that ever wore the McGinnis-inspired "Bluebird" paint scheme, March 1968. Richard E. Anderson photo.

Hinsdale (MP S54.40)

8-5. Ashuelot Branch local, Consolidation 2400 is southbound arriving Hinsdale, Sept. 4, 1948. Albert G. Hale photo; Walker Trans. Coll./Historic Beverly.

8-6. Looking south, a gas car calls Hinsdale, ca. 1950. Donald S. Robinson photo; Walker Trans. Coll./ Historic Beverly.

Ashuelot (MP S58.00)

8-7. Northward view of the "ornamental" Ashuelot station, built in 1882 to replace an earlier station building. Across the tracks, overlooking the station, is the Sheridan House, named after Hugh Sheridan, owner of the Sheridan Manufacturing Co. (textiles, brushed beaver hats), who purchased the home in 1901. Both these structures have survived. The Sheridan House is now the Winchester Historical Society's headquarters and museum, ca. 1905. Matthew D. Cosgro coll.

8-8. Another northward view of the Ashuelot station. Note that one track has been lifted, Oct. 12, 1938. Albert G. Hale photo; R. R. Richards coll.

8-9. Consolidation 2400 southbound with freight, Ashuelot, Sept. 4, 1948. Albert G. Hale photo; Walker Trans. Coll./Historic Beverly.

8-10. Gas car pauses at Ashuelot on its morning run to E. Northfield, ca. 1951. Alan Thomas photo; R. R. Conard coll.

Winchester (MP S60.20)

8-11. Station area at Winchester, Oct. 12, 1938. Albert G. Hale photo; Walker Trans. Coll./Historic Beverly.

8-12. Northward view at Winchester, ca. 1940. Photogr. unknown; Benjamin Campbell coll.

8-13. Consolidation 2400 southbound arriving Winchester, Sept. 4, 1948. Albert G. Hale photo; Walker Trans. Coll./Historic Beverly.

8-14. The 2400 taking water at Winchester, Sept. 4, 1948. Albert G. Hale photo; Walker Trans. Coll./Historic Beverly.

8-15. 2400 south approaching the Rte. 10 crossing between Winchester and W. Swanzey, Sept. 4, 1948. Albert G. Hale photo; Walker Trans. Coll./Historic Beverly.

8-16. Donald S. Robinson photographed trains everywhere, but he didn't just shoot film randomly. As a B&M dispatcher, he had the inside skinny on when and where things were going to happen. Here he photographed what he called E-9, led by two RS3s, at the Rte. 10 crossing between Winchester and W. Swanzey. We believe, based on the date, power, and consist, that E-9 was an early version of EJ-1, an East Deerfield-to-White River Jct. freight, that ran via Keene, May 1963. Walker Trans. Coll./Historic Beverly.

West Swanzey (MP S68.20)

8-17. Here is a wonderful southward view of the scene at West Swanzey, shot from the Christian Hill Road Bridge, showing the station, freight house, and, across the tracks, the New England Box Co. factory, ca. 1940. Today, everything in this image is gone except for the old roadbed and Franklin Mountain. Photog. unknown; Benjamin Campbell coll.

8-18. For years before the coming of train radio, station agents would handwrite or type telegraphed orders received, fasten them to hoops, and pass them up to passing trains—a common practice, yet seldom photographed. Here at West Swanzey station this day, a northbound train has slowed as Agent Guy C. Williams makes ready to "hoop-up" orders. Notice he has two hoops—one for the engine crew and one for the conductor in the buggy, ca. 1940. Photogr. unknown; Benjamin Campbell coll.

Keene (MP S73.70)

8-19. Green Mountain Alco S4 305 crosses Main St. after a spring snowstorm, in what would be the last full year of operations on the Ashuelot Branch. Keene, April 9, 1982. Richard E. Anderson photo.

CHAPTER NINE

THE ASHBURNHAM RAILROAD

The Ashburnham Railroad, backed by citizens determined to connect a modest cluster of industries in Ashburnham Center with the railroad network, was chartered May 5, 1871. The road was built in 1873 from Ashburnham Center ("the Center") to a connection with the Vermont & Massachusetts Railroad in South Ashburnham ("the Junction") and opened January 1, 1874—the same day the Fitchburg leased the V&M. The road declared bankruptcy in 1878, reorganized, and continued independent operations until it sold itself to the Fitchburg in 1885, becoming that system's Ashburnham Branch. The B&M leased the Fitchburg July 1, 1900 and the branch became a part of the B&M system. The road's two major shippers were the Winchester Chair Company in the Center and the W. F. Whitney (Chair) Company at the Junction. Heavy industry in the Center, which had begun a shift to the Junction as early as 1885, was finished in the Center by 1900. Flooding in March 1936 seriously damaged the line, and it was abandoned in 1937.

The Ashburnham was remarkable in a number of respects, starting with its miniature size. The road was only 2.64 miles in length and owned but one locomotive and a combine. In the Center, the road had a brick, two-stall engine house and a station directly in front of it. There was no turning facility there, so the engine always ran forward to the Junction, backwards returning.

For passenger service, the road operated six daily round trips, shuttling passengers between the Center and the Junction. Any freight cars to be moved were added to the passenger trains. The last passenger runs were made on September 2, 1924, after which the B&M substituted a bus. Replacing conventional train service with buses in low-density rural areas was a novel idea at the time, and it was on the little Ashburnham Branch that the B&M first tested the idea.

9-1. A B&M Ashburnham Branch train has just delivered these four intrepid passengers at the South Ashburnham station, where they will probably transfer to a Cheshire Branch train or to a Main Line train on the other side of the station, ca. 1917–1923. The engine will run around the combine and pull it back to Ashburnham Center tender first. Photogr. unknown; James Lane Family Album, Ashburnham Hist. Soc.

9-2. The Ashburnham's 1/*Watatic* at the station, immediately in front of the engine house, with its usual consist—a combine. Ashburnham, ca. 1885. R. Douglas photo; Edna Roy coll.

9-3. The Ashburnham Railroad engine house, built in 1874–1875, in its later life as the town's Public Works Dept. garage. Ashburnham, June 1965. Richard E. Anderson photo.

9-4. Another shot of the old Ashburnham Railroad engine house, Ashburnham, May 3, 1975. It continued as the town's Public Works Dept. garage until 1987, when it collapsed in a snowstorm. Paul M. Pearson photo; B&MRRHS Archives.

CHAPTER 10

THE WORCESTER & CONTOOCOOK ROUTE
East of Monadnock

The Worcester & Contoocook Route was a line of road that gradually formed over a thirty-year period (1848–1878), from four small, originally independent, predecessor roads. These component roads, outward (eastward) from Worcester, were the Boston, Barre & Gardner between Worcester and Winchendon, the Monadnock from Winchendon to Peterboro, the Peterboro & Hillsboro between those two towns, and the Contoocook Valley Railroad from Hillsboro to Contoocook. At Contoocook, connection was made with the Concord & Claremont, over which it was only another twelve miles east to New Hampshire's capital city.

The Concord & Claremont, Peterboro & Hillsboro (P&H), and the Contoocook Valley were always controlled by the Northern Railroad. In 1884, the Boston & Lowell leased the Northern System, setting off a political storm over what was perceived to be a takeover by a foreign road. In 1887, to overcome this difficulty, the powerful Boston & Lowell simply leased itself to the Boston & Maine, a much weaker road but one incorporated in New Hampshire. And that is how, as they say, "the tail came to wag the dog."

Unlike the Northern-controlled P&H and Contoocook Valley, the other two Worcester & Contoocook roads—the Boston, Barre & Gardner and the Monadnock—were controlled by the Fitchburg. On July 1, 1900, the Fitchburg itself fell under the B&M flag when it was leased by that road. Thus, the B&M came to control the entire 84.67-mile Worcester & Contoocook Route. For most of the B&M years, it would be operated as an east–west route, split at Peterboro between its New Hampshire and Fitchburg Divisions. In our treatment, we focus on the 43.81 miles from Gardner to Hillsboro, inclusive.

In many respects, the Worcester & Contoocook was the very essence of a New England country road. Climb-ing into the northern Massachusetts uplands, cresting the Monadnock Plateau in Rindge, New Hampshire, passing lakes and ponds, and finally descending the Contoocook River Valley, it was a route of scenic wonders. Passenger train service operated the full length of the route from Worcester to Contoocook with some trains going through to Concord. Before automobiles, there was a robust summer trade of people traveling to summer homes, camps, and hotels. Wayfreights plied the route, stopping in all the picturesque small towns along the way.

The Worcester & Contoocook, however, struggled to find its place in the B&M system. It was often described as just "a back road to Concord." Unlike the heavier-built, main line-aspiring Cheshire, the Worcester & Contoocook was never destined for glory. By 1925, traffic was already in slow decline as the winds of business and economic change were picking up. In response to competitive pressures and changing consumer demands, small mills that once powered the economy closed or moved out of the area. And, tragically, fire took out many would-be survivors, which never rebuilt.

The route physically began to come apart on March 18, 1936, when torrential rains sent the Contoocook River into a rampage. Floods inflicted severe damage to roadbed and bridges between Peterboro and Hillsboro, ending passenger service east of Peterboro forever. After minimal repairs, limited freight service continued between Peterboro and Elmwood. But effective April 24, 1940, the Worcester & Contoocook main between Elmwood and the Peterboro Yard Limit was taken out of service and subsequently abandoned in 1942. At the same time, five miles of road east of Hillsboro to West Henniker (Emerson) were also abandoned.

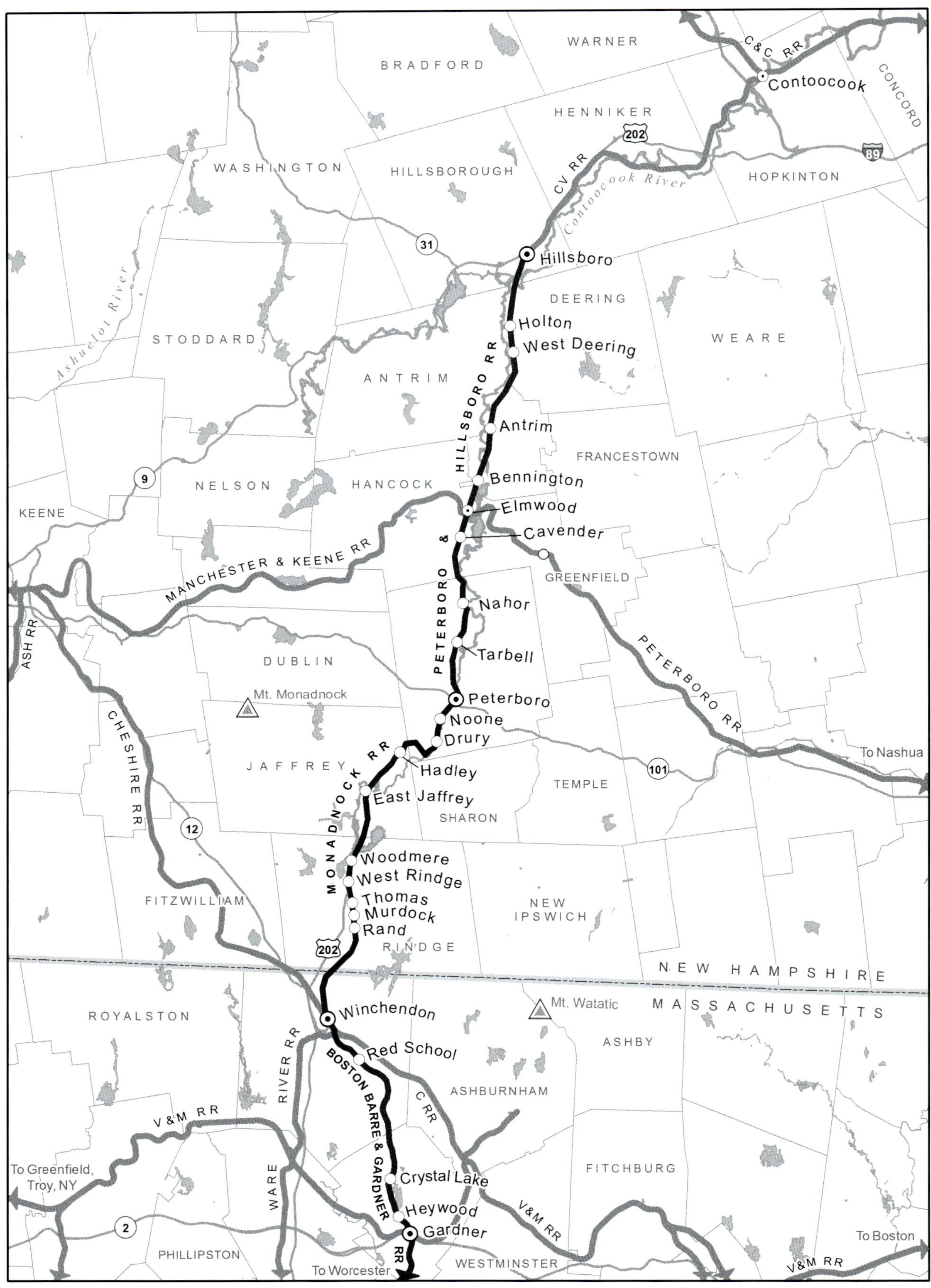
WARNER
BRADFORD
C & C R·R
CONCORD
CONTOOCOOK
Contoocook
HENNIKER
HOPKINTON
89
202
CV RR
Contoocook River
HILLSBOROUGH
WASHINGTON
31
Hillsboro
DEERING
WEARE
Holton
West Deering
STODDARD
Ashuelot River
HILLSBORO RR
ANTRIM
Antrim
FRANCESTOWN
9
KEENE
NELSON
HANCOCK
Bennington
Elmwood
Cavender
MANCHESTER & KEENE RR
GREENFIELD
PETERBORO &
PETERBORO RR
ASH RR
Nahor
DUBLIN
Tarbell
Mt. Monadnock
Peterboro
To Nashua
Noone
Drury
CHESHIRE RR
JAFFREY
MONADNOCK RR
Hadley
101
East Jaffrey
TEMPLE
12
SHARON
Woodmere
West Rindge
Thomas
NEW
Murdock
IPSWICH
FITZWILLIAM
Rand
RINDGE
202
NEW HAMPSHIRE
MASSACHUSETTS
Winchendon
Mt. Watatic
ROYALSTON
Red School
ASHBY
RIVER RR
BOSTON BARRE & GARDNER
ASHBURNHAM
C RR
V & M RR
WARE
To Greenfield,
Troy, NY
FITCHBURG
Crystal Lake
2
Heywood
V & M RR
PHILLIPSTON
Gardner
To Boston
RR
WESTMINSTER
V & M RR
To Worcester

10-1. Country Train 8111, sometimes popularly referred to as the *Blueberry Special*, drawn this day by New Haven Alco RS3 555, is just west of Holden station, headed "upcountry" on its daily M-F, 52-mile trip from Worcester, MA, to Peterboro, NH. The train had recently made its last run with steam on November 18, 1952, after which leased New Haven RS3 diesels had taken over. Late 1952. Berton G. Towle photo.

Now with the line severed in two places, freight and passenger service continued over the western end of the route between Worcester and Peterboro—now called the "Peterboro Branch." But on the eastern end of the route, reaching Hillsboro required creation of the "Hillsboro Branch," that used remaining sections of the Keene Branch from Nashua to Elmwood and the Worcester & Contoocook between Elmwood and Hillsboro. Both the Peterboro and Hillsboro Branches were poignantly recalled as "Mogul Country" branches, where aging Moguls continued to power trains from the mid-1940s to the early 1950s. We discuss the Hillsboro Branch in more detail in the following chapter.

Gardner (MP W26.20)

10-2. Train 8111/Mogul 1402, Gardner, May 6, 1952. Albert G. Hale photo; Walker Trans. Coll./Historic Beverly.

10-4. Train 8111/Mogul 1450, on the Conant St. crossing, approaching the diamond, Gardner, Oct. 1, 1952. Albert G. Hale photo; Walker Trans. Coll./Historic Beverly.

10-5. On the same day, Mogul 1450, on its return trip from Peterboro as Train 8118, makes its station stop at Gardner, Oct. 1, 1952. Albert G. Hale photo; Walker Trans. Coll./Historic Beverly.

We believe the following six Gardner images, now in the B&MRRHS Archives, were probably official B&M photos taken by the Engineering Department in 1959. They show the old Worcester Yard on the Worcester & Contoocook line (compass south of the Peterboro diamonds), in its last days before it was entombed beneath the embankment for the new Rte. 2 in 1961–1963.

10-6a. This image looks south into the Worcester Yard from a point just north of the five-track Conant St. crossing. The photographer's back is to the Gardner Tower. Reference points include the crossing tender's cabin and the ramp across the street that was once used for unloading automobiles. The Peterboro Branch track is at left; the other tracks curving right are leads into the Gardner Yard.

10-6b. Here is a closeup of the automobile ramp seen in the previous photo. Well into the 1940s, new automobiles were shipped directly to local dealerships in large double-door boxcars—four to a car. In time, even before this image was taken, the railroads had begun moving automobiles more efficiently in higher capacity auto rack cars.

10-6c. Now we are at the south end of the yard at the South Main St. crossing, looking north from the crossing tender's cabin. Unlike Conant St., this crossing had gates.

10-6d. The crossing tender at Conant St. was right in the middle of all the action. The Peterboro track is at left, the Fitchburg Main Line at right. Note the orderboards above the Gardner Tower's roof—one for the Peterboro Branch (right), the other for the Main Line.

10-6e. The last days are at hand for the gabled, brick Gardner Station, built in 1895. It had been sold on June 25, 1959 to the Mannos Trust, then leased to Atlantic Refining Co., which demolished it to make way for a gas station on the site.

10-6f. Looking east on Conant St., approaching the Worcester Yard crossings. Worcester is to the right, Peterboro to the left. The Fitchburg Main Line is hidden by parked automobiles but notice the South Main St. overpass at right.

<h1 style="text-align:center">Winchendon (MP W35.98)</h1>

10-7. Train 8118/Mogul 1478 arriving Winchendon, Oct. 15, 1948. Albert G. Hale photo; Walker Trans. Coll./Historic Beverly.

10-8. The head end crew with Train 8111/Mogul 1468. It's "time to go" at Winchendon, ca. 1950. Alan Thomas photo; R. R. Conard coll.

10-9. Mogul 1464 with Train 8118 has just crossed Jackson Ave., and is approaching the Davenport Coal switch, Winchendon, ca. 1952. Photogr. unknown.

10-10. The Davenport Coal Trestle and Shed, Winchendon, winter 1952. Photogr. unknown; B. G. Blodget coll.

10-11. F-7 was a local freight out of Fitchburg. It ran the Cheshire Branch out as far as Troy and made side trips if required to Waterville and Peterboro, before returning to Fitchburg as F-8. One day in Aug. 1968, photographer Richard E. Anderson caught up with F-7 at Winchendon, where he found the power had dropped its train at the "modern" station in Winchendon and gone off to switch a local consignee.

10-12. Not far away he found F-7's head-end, GP7 1563, switching a Monon boxcar for a consignee. Winchendon, Aug. 1968. Richard E. Anderson photo.

10-13. RS2 1500 on the Davenport Coal track, making a switchback move to reach a consignee in the former Converse Toy Co. plant. The Peterboro track is at left, the Cheshire track further left, out of the picture. Winchendon, Jan. 30, 1973. Thomas Murray photo.

10-14. RS2 1500 switching a consignee at the former Converse Toy Co. plant, Winchendon, Jan. 30, 1973. Thomas Murray photo.

10-15. And now the view from the Davenport Coal switch looking southward into the Winchendon yard. It's about 1975 and trains are scarce. Davenport's big coal shed would burn April 23, 1978. Photogr. unknown; B. G. Blodget coll.

West Rindge (MP W41.84)

10-16. West Rindge station, 1935. The agency and side track facility here were discontinued on Oct. 15, 1951, with a provision the waiting room be kept open for passengers. At some point the station was sold and modified into a private home. It burned in 2021 and was demolished in 2022, nothing left. Photogr. unknown; B. G. Blodget coll.

10-17. GP7 1568 eastbound, passes the former station at West Rindge, Aug. 27, 1981. Larry Kemp photo.

East Jaffrey (Jaffrey 1948–) (MP W45.35)

10-18. Looking east on the "business side" of the East Jaffrey station, ca. 1930. Photogr. unknown; Brent S. Michiels coll.

10-19. Train 8118/Mogul 1404 waits in the station while baggage and mail are being handled, as Conductor Mike Downey looks on, Jaffrey, Sept. 8, 1950. Albert G. Hale photo; Walker Trans. Coll./Historic Beverly.

10-20. Approaching Jaffrey station with local F-8, a youthful engineer pilots RS2 1500 over the Rte. 124 crossing, June 1969. Richard E. Anderson photo.

10-21. The 1500, all closed up with nobody around, idles at the old Jaffrey station. It's lunch break. Train crews always knew where the best diners were. June 1969. Richard E. Anderson photo.

10-22. FI-1/GP9R 1821 is just west of the Rte. 124 crossing in Jaffrey. It looks like another lunch break, Aug. 20, 1981. Albert G. Hale photo; Walker Trans. Coll./Historic Beverly.

10-23. A brakeman flags Local 1568 East across Rte. 124, Jaffrey, Aug. 27, 1981. Larry Kemp photo.

10-24. Returning from D. D. Bean's, F-6/GP7 1556 is westbound along Rte. 202 east of Jaffrey near Hill-crest Rd. The line beyond Bean's had been taken out of service in 1969 and Bean's was now the end of the line. D. D. Bean, a maker of matches, used specialty paper in its manufacturing process. The paper, supplied by Fraser Paper of Madawaska, Maine, sometimes moved in the colorful Bangor & Aroostook red-white-and-blue-striped boxcars. Looking well-weathered, the 1556 still wears its original paint—or what's left of it—twenty-two years after it was delivered. July 6, 1972. Larry Kemp photo.

10-25. GP7 1568 is eastbound along Rte. 202, approaching the Hillcrest Rd. crossing east of Jaffrey with cars for D. D. Bean, Aug. 27, 1981. Larry Kemp photo.

Pierce's Crossing (MP W47.02)

10-26. Freight Extra 1451 approaches Pierce's Crossing (at old Rte. 202 between East Jaffrey and Hadley), protected by a "wig-wag" signal. Though used all around the B&M system, especially on branch lines, photos of these early, electric contraptions are not overly common. This particular "wig-wag," in service from at least as early as June 18, 1921, was knocked down twice in its life—last in 1955, shortly after which it was retired (R. Miller, pers. comm.). "Wig-wags" were also installed at the infamous Eastern Ave. crossing in Keene (see Vol. II, p. 141). When activated, in addition to bells and lights, a round disc with the word "stop" would come out of a sleeve and swing back-and-forth. While undoubtedly effective, the "wig-wags" must have been more expensive to maintain than the crossing flashers that replaced them. Signal maintainers must have had a lot of stories about them. ca. 1950. Donald S. Robinson photo; B&MRRHS Archives.

Hadley (MP W47.95)

Not surprisingly for the country road it was, the Worcester & Contoocook had a number of obscure flag stations, many of them named as a nod to landowners who had sold land to the railroad for its right-of-way. Stops at most of these flag stations, at least in later years, were rare occurrences. Between E. Jaffrey and Peterboro alone, there were four—in station order: Pierce's Crossing, Hadley, Drury, and Noone. They all had a sign and a flag signal, but only Noone could boast a small station building. The others probably at one time had little three-sided shelters, but we have never seen a picture showing this for any of them.

10-27. Train 8111/Mogul 1427 at Hadley. Note the station sign and flag stop signal, undated. Donald S. Robinson photo (assigned); B. G. Blodget coll.

10-29. F-8/Alco S1 1170 on bridge W48.42, just across Rte. 202 east of Hadley, June 1967. Richard E. Miller photo.

10-30. Richard E. Anderson has caught up again with F-7/GP7 1563 at bridge W48.42, just across Rte. 202 east of Hadley, Aug. 1968.

(*opposite page*) 10-28. Alco S3 1185 is running eastward along old Rte. 202 at Hadley, Aug. 16, 1956. Donald S. Robinson photo; Walker Trans. Coll./Historic Beverly.

Noone (MP W50.48)

10-31. F-7's passage alongside Rte. 202 proves to any skeptic that there really are tracks here. Noone, Aug. 1968. Richard E. Anderson photo.

Peterboro (MP W51.90)

10-32. Peterboro depot, ca. 1940. Photogr. unknown; Benjamin Campbell coll.

10-33. This is the west end of the Peterboro Engine House. After the floods of 1936 ended through service on the Worcester & Contoocook, Peterboro was no longer a connection point for the Fitchburg and New Hampshire Divisions, nor a home terminal for trains and crews. The track between Elmwood and the Peterboro Yard Limit was retired April 24, 1940, and abandoned in 1942. The need for any layover facilities at Peterboro thus obviated, the engine house was retired in 1942 and was gone by 1945. The turntable (left, out of the picture) was used into 1953 and was removed June 12, 1957 (L. Kemp, pers. comm.). Photogr. unknown; Dale O. Russell coll.

10-34. Train 8118/Mogul 1448, all set to depart for Worcester at 1:05. Commenting on the scene, the photographer noted, "nothing changed here for fifty years until the train was taken off." Peterboro, ca. 1950. Alan Thomas photo; R. R. Conard coll.

10-35. Three Budd RDC-1s (6152, 6107, and 6105) called Peterboro on a RRE excursion June 8, 1958. Led by gleaming, almost-new 6152, the trip marked the only time B&M Budds ever ran into Peterboro. The 6105, on the opposite end of the train, led back to Boston. The station here was razed in 1961 and it is difficult for visitors to the square today to visualize exactly where the station once stood. Fortunately the Peterborough Diner hasn't moved and serves as a good reference point. Photogr. unknown; Brent S. Michiels coll.

10-36. Images such as this one recall the days when boxcars, sporting the liveries of far-away roads, roamed the country. There were still a great many independent roads—roads now among the "fallen flags." Here we see two foreign cars spotted at the Peterborough Basket Co., ca. 1965. Photogr. unknown; Benjamin Campbell coll.

10-37. F-7/Alco S1 1170 switching at Peterboro, June 1967. Richard E. Miller photo.

10-38 & 10-39. F-7 has made it to Peterboro, where the crew prepares to run around the train (above) and to spot a Wabash boxcar on the public delivery track (below), Aug. 1968. Richard E. Anderson photos.

10-40. On one of the last trips to run all the way to Peterboro, RS3 1506 has arrived with three carloads of steel, shown here being off-loaded at the Rte. 101 crossing. The steel was for the gymnasium at the Con-Val Regional High School, then under construction in Peterboro, May 16, 1969. It would be one of the last trips to run all the way to Peterboro. ICC Docket No. 25993 revealed that by August 1969, freight traffic had eroded so badly that only twenty loads had been delivered to Peterboro in the preceding eighteen months. The line was taken out of service the following year. Larry Kemp photo.

Elmwood (Hancock Junction) (MP W59.13)

(see pictures and discussion in Chapter 13, pages 181-187)

Bennington (MP W61.25)

10-41. Train 35/American 710 at the station at Bennington, pre-1911. Photogr. unknown; B. G. Blodget coll.

Antrim (MP W63.19)

10-42. Steam fills the air as derricks are working a derailment that had three cars down the embankment here, about a quarter mile west of Antrim station, Feb. 17, 1922 (see Vol. II, p. 84). It appears a coach has been lifted out of the snow and is back on the iron. Dale O. Russell coll.

Hillsboro (MP W70.01)

(see more pictures and discussion in Chapter 11)

10-43. Spit-and-polished B&M American 790 at the Hillsboro engine house, ca. 1890. Al Pillsbury photo; Benjamin Campbell coll.

10-44. Hillsboro station and yard. Note the team track along Depot St. in this and the following image, ca. 1910. Photogr. unknown; B. G. Blodget coll.

10-45. Slightly broader view of Hillsboro's railroad facilities, showing the 50,000-gallon water tank at the extreme right. The tank was retired in 1943, the year after through traffic on the Worcester & Contoocook ended. The road continued to purchase water from the town, without the expense of maintaining the tank, ca. 1910. Photogr. unknown; B. G. Blodget coll.

10-46. A young woman poses next to the north portal of the Hillsboro Covered Bridge (W69.67). The pedestrian walkway at right was for the convenience of workers at the Contoocook Mills, located across the river from the village, ca. 1905–1910. Postcard; B. G. Blodget coll.

CHAPTER ELEVEN

THE HILLSBORO BRANCH, 1942–
Nashua–Greenfield (MP N26.86)–Hillsboro (MP N43.15)

After the B&M abandoned sections of the Worcester & Contoocook Route in 1942, the only option left for reaching Hillsboro was from Nashua. Hence, the 43.15 mile "Hillsboro Branch" was born. Trains on the 16.29-mile outer end of the branch beyond Greenfield used cobbled together remnants of the former Keene and Worcester & Contoocook Branches. In 1943, the name of the entire branch from Nashua out to Hillsboro was officially changed to the Hillsboro Branch. All the mile posts and bridge numbers beyond Elmwood to Hillsboro were recalculated to reflect mileage from Nashua (see Vol. II, pp. 38, 87). As a New Hampshire Division branch, trains running toward Hillsboro were timetable outward/northward, toward Nashua timetable inward/southward. Connection of the two lines was initially made at Elmwood, using the diamond or (after 1948) a "shoe-fly." But in 1952, "Magoon's Curve" was commissioned to directly connect the two lines, allowing continuous operation, bypassing Elmwood. The name of the bypass recognized section foreman Eddie Magoon, who went down in history as having originated the idea.

The Hillsboro Branch was counted among a cluster of the B&M's rural branch lines fondly remembered as "Mogul Country" for the 2-6-0 Mogul steam engines that puffed along the routes into the early 1950s. (The Peterboro Branch, discussed in the previous chapter, was another "Mogul Country" branch in the Monadnock Region—one, in fact, of particular note because of its passenger train.) In steam days, Hillsboro Branch trains originated at the Middlesex Engine House (between Lowell and North Chelmsford, Massachusetts) and would run up to Nashua and then out the branch, all the way to Hillsboro. Two daily, local freights—one each way—worked the branch, switching consignees' sidings and meeting at different points depending on the amount of work they

had along the way. The outward train overnighted at Hillsboro. Though the Hillsboro roundhouse had burned in 1939, the turntable was still used all the time to spin the Moguls. The last steam run on the branch was N-2/1458 that departed Hillsboro for Nashua on February 28, 1952. The turntable was retired about 1959.

Dieselization brought about major operational changes. The opposing trains were replaced by a single Monday–Saturday peddler freight that ran out from Nashua and back the same day, working consignees' sidings all along the forty-three-mile route. The train would routinely get as far as Greenfield and then continue on to Bennington and Hillsboro as traffic conditions warranted. Over the years, the job was symbolized in different ways, but for consistency in our captions, we use N-1 for the outward/northward side of the job, N-2 for the inward/southward side.

Only diesels no heavier than Alco and EMD 1100-series switchers were allowed on the branch on account of a weight restriction placed on a long, high bridge—the Gulf Viaduct—south of Greenfield in South Lyndeborough. Conveniently, the crews almost always ran north cab forward and south long-hood forward, making it easy to tell the direction a train is headed in images of these diesel switchers on the branch. Heavier diesels quickly appeared on the branch after the Gulf Viaduct was replaced by a new bridge in 1982.

In 1973, the B&M, citing ice and deteriorated track conditions, abruptly took the eight and a half miles of road north of Bennington to Hillsboro out of service—and abandoned them in 1979. The last regular freight to run all the way through to Hillsboro operated New Year's Eve, 1972, dropping two loads of oil and lifting two empties at Vaillancourt Oil. Months later, a light move to Hillsboro was made to retrieve the two oil cars that had been left behind (Bruce Davison, pers. comm.).

After it had not felt a train for more than a decade, the Hillsboro Covered Bridge was torched by an arsonist and destroyed Oct. 30, 1983. Then in 1984, the B&M was acquired by Guilford Rail System, which embargoed the line from Wilton out to Bennington and proposed to abandon it. In 1988, however, the state purchased and "railbanked" the line beyond Wilton and leased it to the Milford-Bennington Railroad. Though the line is not abandoned, demand for rail service beyond Wilton has not materialized.

Greenfield (MP N26.86)

11-1. N-2, this day with Alco S3 1180 in charge, passing Zephyr Lake, Greenfield, July 8, 1965. Richard E. Anderson photo.

11-2. E. C. & W. L. Hopkins/Granite State Feeds, Slip Rd., Greenfield, Feb. 1968. Richard E. Anderson photo.

11-3. N-1/SW1 1132, Greenfield, June 1969. Richard E. Anderson photo.

11-4. Fire drill at the E. C. & W. L. Hopkins grain mill, Slip Rd., Greenfield, 1972. Unfortunately, the drill didn't alter the course of history—the mill took fire around 3:30 a.m., June 27, 1976, and developed into a huge blaze. It was seen for miles and miles around and required several days to extinguish. The mill was never rebuilt. At the time, the B&M station agent's office was located in the mill and all the station records were lost in the blaze. The road suffered a major loss of traffic, which no doubt hastened the end of service on the outer end of the branch. Larry Kemp photo.

11-5. N-1/SW1 1122 at Slip Rd., Greenfield, Nov. 1972. Larry Kemp photo.

11-6. N-1/SW1 1132 is on the way out to Vaillancourt Oil in Hillsboro with a Saturday oil delivery, Greenfield, Dec. 16, 1972. Larry Kemp photo.

11-7. N-1, this day with "blue-dipped" SW1 1129 and matching buggy C135, Greenfield, May 14, 1973. Richard E. Anderson photo.

11-8. N-1/1129 plowing its way out to Bennington at Forest Road (Rte. 136), Greenfield, Feb. 7, 1975. Larry Kemp photo.

11-9. The siding at E. C. & W. L. Hopkins grain mill was double-ended and would often be switched by N-1 on its way out and N-2 on its way home. Here we see N-1/1129 switching the mill, Greenfield, Nov. 25, 1975. Larry Kemp photo.

11-10. N-2/MEC GP38 566 just north of Greenfield State Park. At this time, the B&M had joined the Maine Central in the Guilford Rail System and the two roads' power was already being mixed. Oct. 1983. Larry Kemp photo.

11-11. N-1/GP9R 1806 approaching Slip Rd. crossing. The prefabricated garage structure at left—on the site once occupied by the grain mill—is now Sullivan Bros. Paving. Greenfield, Jan. 1985. Larry Kemp photo.

11-12. Milford-Bennington Railroad SW9 901 (ex-Canadian National 7951)—making a rare appearance in Greenfield—is parked alongside Rte. 136 for the Greenfield Railroad Show, Oct. 19, 2013. B. G. Blodget photo.

Elmwood (MP N32.27)

(see pictures and discussion in Chapter 13, pages 181-187)

Bennington (MP N34.39)

11-13. In Volume II, page 89, we showed Brent Michiels' image of SW1 1122 stranded in Hillsboro. This image shows why it was stranded there: the charred remains of the Bennington Covered Bridge (N34.54) the day after it burned, May 1, 1965. The B&M Engineering Dept. quickly replaced the bridge with a wooden trestle with steel stringers. Richard E. Anderson photo.

11-14. Materials and some interesting equipment at Bennington Depot, a staging point during the Bennington Covered Bridge replacement project, May 1965. Alan Thomas photo; Benjamin Campbell coll.

11-15. N-1/1132, crossing the new bridge, June 1969. Richard E. Anderson photo.

11-16. N-2/1132, headed home the same day with a Southern boxcar, June 1969. Richard E. Anderson photo.

11-17. N-1/1129, along Rte. 202 at Powder Mill Pond, Bennington, undated. Alan Thomas photo; Benjamin Campbell coll.

11-19. N-2/1129 headed home along Rte. 202 at Powder Mill Pond, undated. Alan Thomas photo; Benjamin Campbell coll.

11-18. N-1/1129 switching Monadnock Paper, Bennington, undated. Alan Thomas photo; Benjamin Campbell coll.

11-20. Passenger Extra B&M RDC-2 6212 on the Bennington Bridge. It's a New Hampshire Public Utilities Commission inspection train. Nov. 7, 1973. Richard E. Anderson photo.

11-21. Rerailing the plow at the paper mill switch, Bennington, undated. Alan Thomas photo; Benjamin Campbell coll.

11-22. N-2/1129 returning light to Nashua, passes Powder Mill Pond, Bennington, Feb. 6, 1975. Larry Kemp photo.

11-23. On another day, N-2 is plowing its way home, Bennington, undated. Alan Thomas photo; Benjamin Campbell coll.

11-24. Because there was no run-around track at Bennington, the RRE's *Crotched Mountain Limited* ran out the branch with the train arranged push–pull—MBTA 1002 leading five ex-B&M "Boise Budd" cars northbound, 1006 leading southbound. You can see the whole train in this image, northbound approaching the boat launch road crossing at Otter Lake, Greenfield State Park, April 23, 1983. Bruce Davison photo.

11-25. MBTA 1006 with the RRE excursion train at the depot, Bennington, April 23, 1983. The excursion marked one of the first trips on the branch beyond Wilton with heavier power following replacement of the Gulf Viaduct in Lyndeborough with a new bridge in 1982. Larry Kemp photo.

11-26. The southbound *Crotched Mountain Limited* led by MBTA 1006, poses at Powder Mill Pond with its namesake mountain beyond. Bennington, April 23, 1983. Larry Kemp photo.

11-27. MBTA 1006 swings into Magoon's Curve with the southbound *Crotched Mountain Limited*, Elmwood, April 23, 1983. Bruce Davison photo.

11-28. N-2/GP9 1707 at the depot, Bennington, Oct. 12, 1984. Larry Kemp photo.

11-29. N-2/GP18 1755 at Powder Mill Pond, Bennington, March 11, 1985. Larry Kemp photo.

Antrim (MP N36.33)

11-30. Though the freight house siding remains in place, the house itself looks like its days are about over. Antrim, undated. Alan Thomas photo; Benjamin Campbell coll.

West Deering (MP N39.44)

11-31. The sweet twilight has caught N-1/1122 opening the line after a heavy snowfall. Photographer Richard E. Anderson noted that taking pictures on the outer end of the branch could be frustrating because sometimes N-1, working its way out from Nashua, would not show up until good light had begun to fade. For your bearings, that is Crotched Mountain off to the southeast. West Deering, Feb. 28, 1972.

Hillsboro (MP N43.15)

To persons unfamiliar with the railroad in Hillsboro—which nowadays is most of us—visualizing the railroad's layout in the town from pictures alone can be difficult. For example, pictures of the Hillsboro Covered Bridge (N42.63) and the trestle—and their relationship to each other—can be confusing since the structures were large enough that it was impossible to get them both in the same frame. Bear in mind, trains coming into Hillsboro first crossed the covered bridge, then crossed Bridge Street (Rte. 149) at grade, and then traversed the long curving trestle. River Street passed beneath the trestle. In another half-mile, railroad facilities consisting of a small yard, a 50,000-gallon water tank, and the passenger station, freight house, and engine house—were reached. All the railroad structures were located on the west side of the tracks, except for the water tank, which was situated on the east side of the tracks, just south of the station.

(*opposite page*)11-32. This image, taken on a RRE trip, looks north from the open platform of an old wooden coach. Local freight N-1 is on the freight house siding, probably laying over until the following morning. Hillsboro, June 29, 1947. Photogr. unknown; Larry Kemp coll.

11-33. Mogul 1455 on the turntable lead. Depot St. is at left. The Vaillancourt Oil facilities are visible beyond, at the end of the line. Hillsboro, ca. 1948. Photogr. unknown; Benjamin Campbell coll.

11-34. Mogul 1487 at the turntable, Hillsboro, ca. 1949. Glenn A. Wagner photo; Brent S. Michiels coll.

11-35. This view is looking north in the Hillsboro Yard at the end of the Hillsboro Branch, 1951. The Mogul has been turned on the turntable (north of the freight house) and is heading south. The weather-beaten station was closed after flooding ended passenger service north of Peterboro in 1936, but the railroad retained the land and passenger station until finally selling it in 1960. Philip R. Hastings photo; California State Railroad Library Archives.

11-36. N-1, threading its way into the village, has just crossed Bridge St. (Rte. 149) and is on the trestle, about to cross over River St. When the Peterboro & Hillsboro was built in 1876–1878, construction work required to get the road into Hillsboro made it the most challenging section of the road to build. Hillsboro, ca. 1955. Alan Thomas photo; Benjamin Campbell coll.

11-37. Crew on N-1/1124 are preparing to stop and protect at Bridge St. (Rte. 149) just north of the covered bridge, Hillsboro, ca. 1966. Photogr. unknown; Benjamin Campbell coll.

11-38. Now N-1 is on the trestle and will cross River St. above grade and continue on northward into the yard. Hillsboro, ca. 1966. Photogr. unknown; Benjamin Campbell coll.

11-39. In this frigid scene, while N-1/1124 is switching Vaillancourt Oil, two crewmen are busy shoveling accumulated snow off the plow. They will certainly need it this day. Hillsboro, undated. Alan Thomas photo; Benjamin Campbell coll.

11-40. Clearing the yard after what appears to have been a pretty good nor'easter. When it's time for some coffee and a hot meal, the nearby presence of the Hillsboro Diner (extreme left) is not lost on the crew. Hillsboro, undated. Alan Thomas photo; Benjamin Campbell coll.

11-41. Departing Hillsboro, N-2/1124 will plow its way back to Nashua. Undated. Alan Thomas photo; Benjamin Campbell coll.

11-42. The Hillsboro Covered Bridge (N42.63), looking upstream. The trestle would be to the right (timetable north), out of the picture, Feb. 1970. Richard E. Anderson photo.

11-43. N-1/1132 emerges from the bridge, Hillsboro, Feb. 1970. Richard E. Anderson photo.

11-44. N-1/1132 on the trestle above River St. with its short train, Hillsboro, Feb. 1970. Richard E. Anderson photo.

11-45. Now at the north end of the yard, N-1 is switching cars for Vaillancourt Oil, the last large customer in Hillsboro, Feb. 1970. Richard E. Anderson photo.

11-46. N-1/1122, the same train we saw back at West Deering, is now on the trestle, coming into town, Feb. 28, 1972. At the end of the year, B&M, citing ice build-up and deteriorated track conditions, abruptly ended service north of Bennington—and never resumed service. Richard E. Anderson photo.

CHAPTER TWELVE

THE WARE RIVER RAILROAD
"The Albany Road"

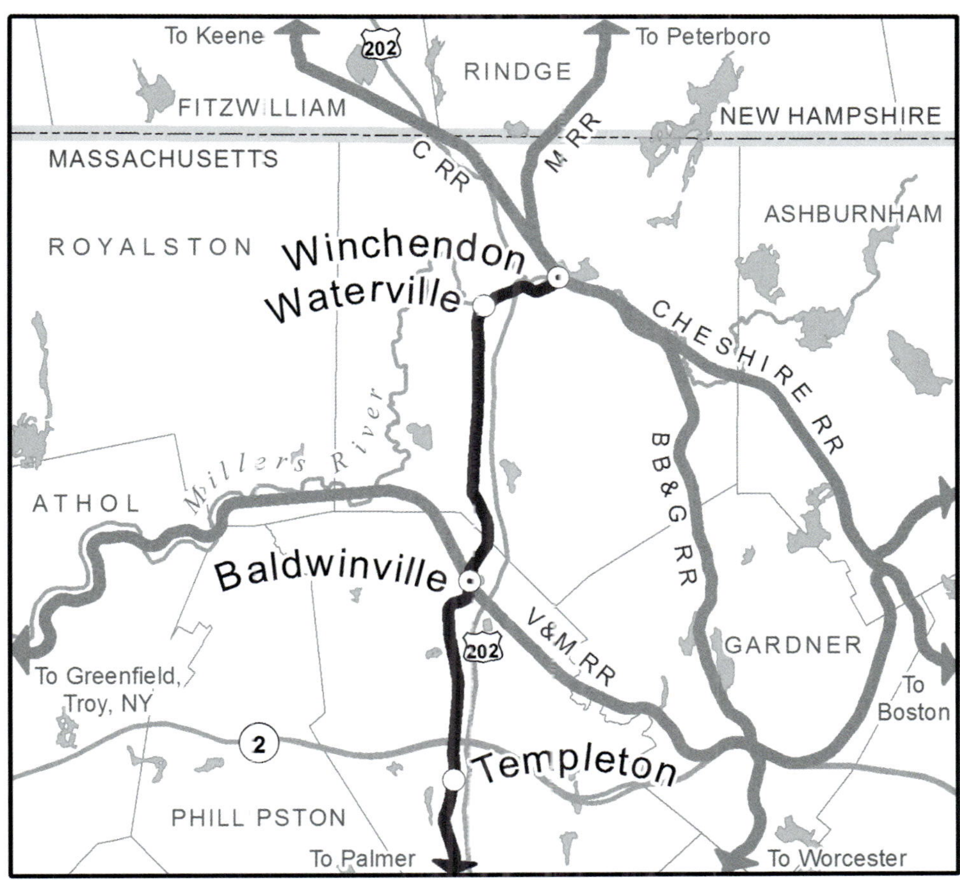

The Ware River Railroad was originally chartered in 1851, then rechartered in 1867, to build from a connection with the Boston & Albany (B&A) at Palmer to Winchendon. For its first twenty-five miles the road followed the Ware River Valley, then the Millers River Valley beyond to Winchendon. Construction of the road began in 1868 and it was built northward in sections, opening to Winchendon in December 1873. The road was 49.4 miles in length. Only the road's outermost 10.4 miles reached into the Monadnock Region, with stations at Templeton, Baldwinville, Waterville, and Winchendon.

The Ware River was a single-track, unsignaled road. It made diamond crossings of the Vermont & Massachusetts at Baldwinville and the Cheshire at Winchendon. Terminal facilities at Winchendon included a small yard, turntable, roundhouse, passenger station, and freight house. The high, 1,050-foot long Otter River Bridge in Baldwinville was the most notable structure on the entire line.

The B&A, alarmed by the prospect another road could acquire the Ware River and divert traffic at Springfield, leased the road in January 1874. The road became its Ware River (or Winchendon) Branch. It was the longest branch and Winchendon the northernmost station on the B&A system. In 1900, the B&A was itself leased by the New York Central (NYC), which carried the road on its books as an unconsolidated subsidiary. It was not fully merged until 1961.

12-1. The B&A's three-stall roundhouse and turntable in Winchendon. We believe these facilities were destroyed by flooding in 1936 and were never rebuilt. After their loss, trains returned to Palmer tender-first. Undated. Photogr. unknown; Narragansett Hist. Soc.

12-2. There were a lot of Otter River Bridges. This image shows the B&A's 1,050-foot steel-lattice bridge over the river in Baldwinville. It's an unusual view, showing the B&M's twin 50,000-gallon water tanks across the river on its main line, east of the B&A diamond, ca. 1910. Harry Aldrich coll.

12-3. NYC *Beeliners* being flagged across Spring St. on the *Ware River Rocket* excursion. Just look at the cab, packed with children and fans. Passengers recalled it didn't seem to bother the engineer at all, Winchendon, May 5, 1962. Photogr. unknown; Benjamin Campbell coll.

12-4. The *Ware River Rocket* crosses the B&A bridge by Whitney Pond, as it nears the end of the line, Winchendon, May 5, 1962. Photogr. unknown; Benjamin Campbell coll.

The Great Hurricane of September 21, 1938, nearly wiped out the Ware River Branch. The branch was damaged so severely the NYC considered abandonment, but ultimately restored the line after a six-week outage. Passenger service between Palmer and Winchendon ended July 27, 1948, although the daily freight would carry a trailing combine to accommodate a robust less-than-carload and parcel post business (but no passengers) into 1960. In the Monadnock Region, the mainstay customers were always chairmakers, other furnituremakers, and woodenware industries. The B&A competed fiercely with the B&M for carloads at Baldwinville and Winchendon, where both roads flourished together—but also died together—as economic changes, the closure or departure of industries, and trucks sapped away their life blood.

After its 1961 merger into the NYC, the road began to contemplate abandoning the Ware River Branch north of South Barre, but service continued. Then, upon the merger of the bankrupt NYC and Pennsylvania Railroads on February 1, 1968, the Ware River Branch became a remote outpost on the sprawling PennCentral system. The PennCentral quickly abandoned the twenty-three miles of road from South Barre to Waterville and tore up the track. It sold the outermost two miles from Waterville to Winchendon to the B&M, which operated it as its Waterville Branch/Industrial Track to reach the New England Wooden Ware Co. mill. Local freights from Fitchburg ran out cobbled-together remnants of the Cheshire and Peterboro Branches (named the Monadnock Branch after 1977) and made side trips to Waterville as needed. The Monadnock Branch was abandoned in 1984.

12-5. Remains of the B&A/NYC station, Winchendon, Sept. 24, 1966. Richard E. Miller photo.

12-6. PennCentral/NYC Train LC-5 with Alco RS3 5523 northbound at Baldwinville. The B&A's freight house is at right, the B&M's beyond. June 25, 1968. Richard E. Miller photo.

12-7. PennCentral/NYC Train LC-5 didn't spend much time in Winchendon. It would normally do its work and be ready to depart in about an hour. Here Alco RS3 5240 is running around its train. Over at the far left is the B&M's freight house across Central St., Winchendon, Aug. 1968. Richard E. Miller photo.

12-8. Alco RS3 5240 has finished its work and is all ready to depart Winchendon as Train LC-6, Aug. 1968. Richard E. Miller photo.

12-9. FI-1/GP9R 1821 crosses the diamond as it begins a side trip down the Waterville Branch. In the branch's last years, it was downgraded to an industrial track. Winchendon, Aug. 20, 1981. Albert G. Hale photo; Walker Trans. Coll./Historic Beverly.

12-10. Here we see FI-1 has arrived Benjamin (Depot) St. and the engineer and conductor are discussing the switching moves to be made at Waterville. Aug. 20, 1981. Albert G. Hale photo; Walker Trans. Coll./Historic Beverly.

12-11. FI-1 switching the New England Wooden Ware plant, Waterville, Aug. 20, 1981. Albert G. Hale photo; Walker Trans. Coll./Historic Beverly.

CHAPTER THIRTEEN

THE MANCHESTER & KEENE RAILROAD

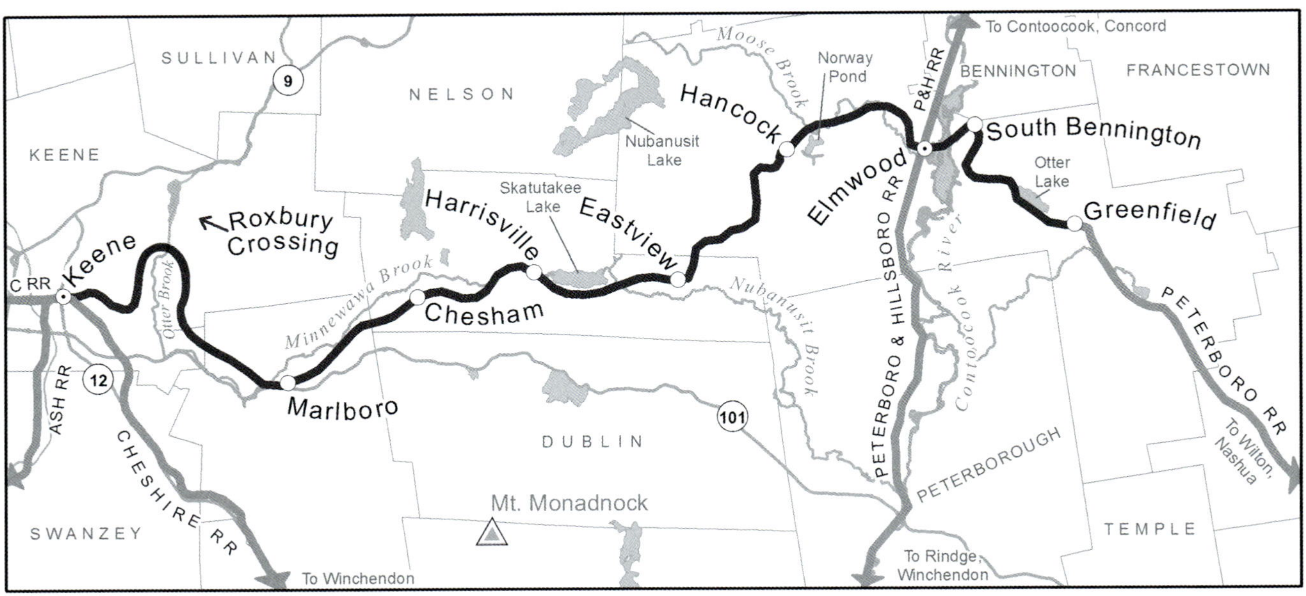

The Manchester and Keene Railroad (M&K) was the last new railroad built in the Monadnock Region—and it was the first to be abandoned. Chartered June 22, 1864—during the Civil War—nearly twelve years passed before the first spade of earth was turned. Construction began May 15, 1876 and the 29.6-mile line, from a connection with the Peterborough Railroad at Greenfield to Keene, was completed November 29, 1878. It was arranged that the Nashua & Lowell Railroad (N&L) would operate the road, and service began in early December 1878. Due to washouts and other problems, however, service was on-again, off-again for about a year before the N&L gave up and discontinued service.

In early 1880, the M&K went bankrupt. The receivers contracted with the Connecticut River Railroad to operate the road and service was restored on September 1, 1880. A 50-50 consortium consisting of the Concord and the Boston & Lowell (B&L) Railroads purchased the road at the bankruptcy sale on October 26, 1881 and took charge of the road at the start of 1882. The road was effectively operated by the B&L, as the outer end of its Keene Branch. In its first five years, the B&L invested heavily, rebuilding much of the M&K's original infrastructure. Then in 1887, the B&L leased itself to the B&M. The lease gave the B&M its first entry into the Monadnock Region and—via its connection with the Cheshire at Keene—an east–west route of some importance to the Connecticut River at Bellows Falls. Its early importance as an east–west route faded rapidly after the B&M leased the Fitchburg system in 1900.

For most of the B&M years, the M&K was operated as a timetable north–south road. It was a single-iron, unsignalized road, with operations governed by train orders. There were passing tracks at all stations. By 1930, the road had entirely 75-pound rail, except for 2.4 miles of 100-pound rail laid in 1927. There were fifty numbered bridges, including about a mile of open, wooden

13-1a & 1b. Corporate embosser of the Manchester & Keene Railroad, Incorporated 1864. B. G. Blodget coll.

trestles. In the road's first decade, many of the open trestles were shortened by filling and all were ironized. There were ninety-seven curves (about half the road was curved) and many severe grades. The road's highest elevation was 1,253 feet, reached at MP44 north of Harrisville. Northward, from the Contoocook River Bridge (N31.81) to the summit, the road rose 568 feet in twelve miles; Southward from Keene to the summit, the road climbed 775 feet in thirteen miles. The ruling grade northbound was 1.88 percent, southbound 2.40 percent.

The population along the line was sparse; in the 1930 United States Census, Keene had a population of 13,794; Marlborough 1,508; Hancock 561; and Harrisville 512. Prior to January 9, 1934, two sets of passenger trains (8218/8219 and 8224/8225) ran weekdays, a pattern that had continued uninterrupted from the turn of the century. In a 1933 random thirty-day sample, passengers per day between Keene and Elmwood for the two sets of trains averaged 3.7/5.4 and 10.2/5.3, respectively. Until January 9, 1934, a local freight operated three days a week, running out from Elmwood, each time only as far as traffic required.

The road's best years were 1890–1910, when agricultural traffic and manufacturing traffic—notably from textile and woodenware mills—were strong. But by 1915, freight traffic was already in decline due to changing economic conditions. Manufacturing businesses—

faced with increasing competition from other parts of the country—closed or moved away, agricultural traffic went into decline as farms were abandoned, and truck competition began to be felt.

As early as December 1924, the B&M had filed with the ICC for permission to abandon the Keene Branch between Elmwood and Keene, but the request was denied. Operations continued until January 9, 1934, when the filled Moose Brook Trestle (N35.30) south of Hancock station washed out, severing the line. Passenger service ended and never resumed. Limited freight service from Keene as far as Hancock continued until May 1, 1935, when it was discontinued. The B&M and its truck and bus subsidiary, the B&M Transportation Company, agreed to continue service to Marlboro by truck. Up until the time operations were abandoned, Marlboro had remained the busiest station on the line, providing 40 percent of its total freight (coal, wooden boxes, and less-than-carload business). At Harrisville, Colony Mills (textiles) was the only remaining customer. Historically it had consumed 1,500 to 2,000 tons of coal per year, but that amount had fallen off in the last ten years due to slumping business and subnormal operations.

Service continued out from Elmwood, north about two miles to Coolidge Crossing (Mill Road) in Hancock, to accommodate Hancock businesses. Then came the September 1938 hurricane, which delivered the coup de grâce, further damaging the line and ending service to Coolidge Crossing. The 21.9 miles of track from Keene to Coolidge Crossing was abandoned in 1938, followed by 1.8 miles of track from Elmwood to Coolidge Crossing in 1939. In 1940, the B&M tore up the whole line between Keene and Elmwood, except for a short spur at Elmwood that was used for switching trains to and from the Hillsboro Branch. Remaining Manchester & Keene trackage between Greenfield and Elmwood was incorporated into the Hillsboro Branch in 1942.

Greenfield (MP N26.86)

13-2. A snow train has arrived at Greenfield from Boston, and winter sports enthusiasts of every stripe have alighted for a day of winter fun. Pack Monadnock Mountain looms in the distance, partly obscured in the clouds of steam. The train will continue on to Elmwood where it will turn on the wye. 1935. Dale O. Russell coll; used by permission of Hillsborough Hist. Soc., the copyright holder.

13-3. USGS topographic map (1900) showing Elmwood, junction of the B&M's Keene and Peterboro & Hillsboro Branches. Notice Rte. 202 did not exist at this time.

Elmwood (Hancock Junction) (MP N32.27 and MP W59.13)

At Elmwood, the Manchester & Keene Railroad and the Peterboro & Hillsboro Railroad (in B&M years, the Keene Branch and the Worcester & Contoocook Branch respectively) crossed each other on a diamond. The crossing was protected by a manual ball signal system that was simply a tall mast with two pulleys—one pulley raised and lowered a single ball; the other pulley, two balls. One ball displayed gave Keene Branch trains the right to cross the diamond, two balls Worcester & Contoocook trains.

As the crossing point for the two lines, Elmwood was, of course, a train order station. Its chief functions and infrastructure were to move trains safely through the junction and to supply passing trains with water and coal. It has sometimes been referred to as a "railroad village," but this may be a bit of a stretch. Though farms dotted the surrounding countryside, nobody, save the station agent and family members, lived at Elmwood. Passengers changing between connecting trains used the station, but few passenger trips actually originated or terminated at Elmwood. Freight traffic handled or interchanged at Elmwood was similarly very limited. Freight business never warranted a dedicated freight house. Residents and businesses in all the surrounding towns—Hancock, Bennington, Peterboro, and Greenfield—all had their own, very adequate passenger and freight facilities.

The coaling facility at Elmwood was retired in 1926,

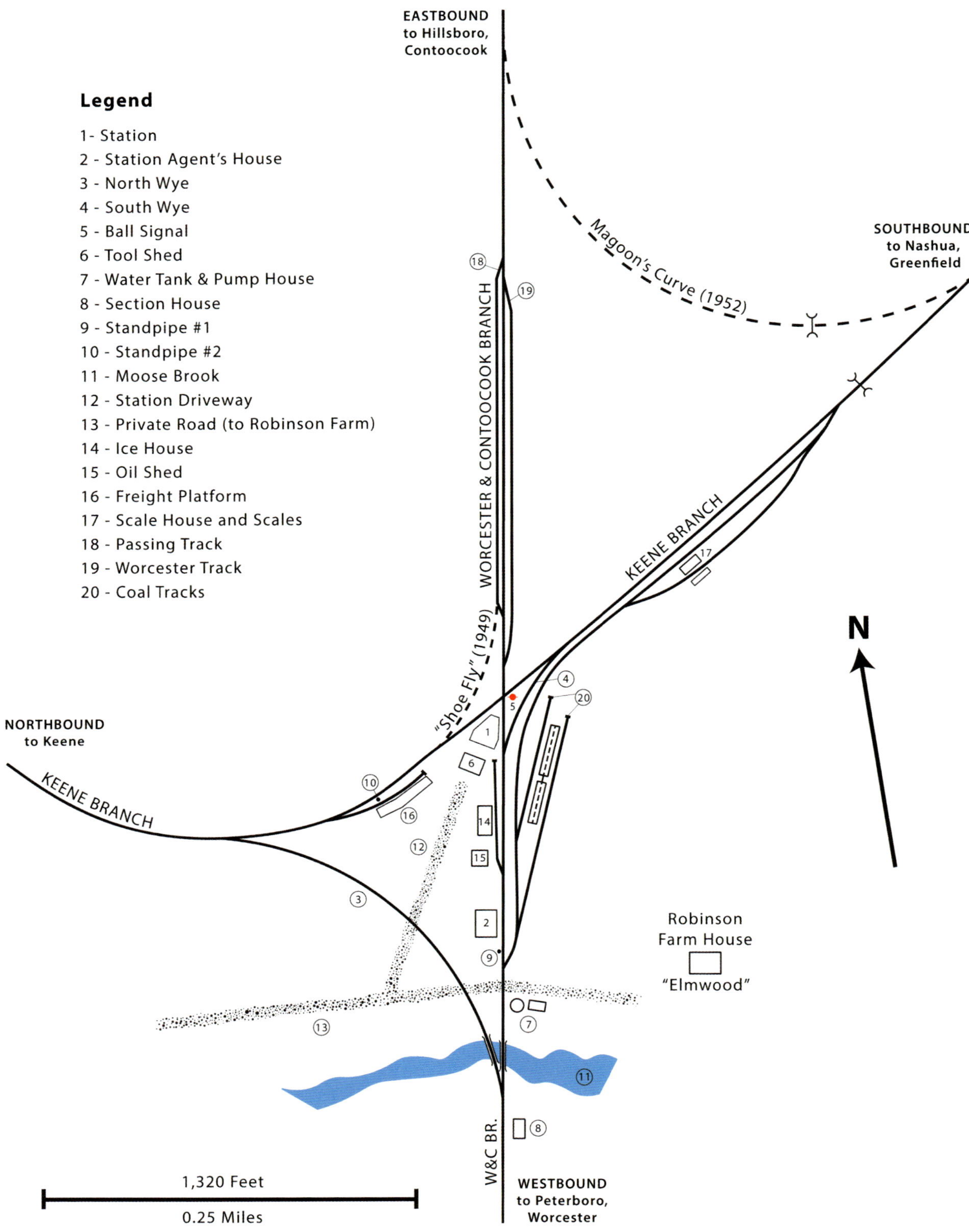

13-4. Composite track diagram showing points of interest at Elmwood, NH, 1900–1952. Not all tracks are shown and tracks and structures shown did not necessarily all exist at the same time. After Magoon's Curve was commissioned in 1952, all then-remaining track at Elmwood was retired. Railroad directions shown are timetable directions, not compass directions. Map adapted from Symmes & Hornsby, *B&M Bulletin* 4(1), no. 1 (1974): 10–19.

the station master's house in 1934. By 1942, through traffic on both lines had ended and Elmwood was done. The water tank was retired in 1942 and demolished the following year. Use of ball signals at Elmwood was discontinued on October 13, 1943, and the station building was demolished about 1945.

A helpful rule for getting oriented when viewing Elmwood images, is to always remember that the station building stood in the *compass southwest* quadrant of the crossing, the ball signal in the *compass southeast* quadrant of the crossing.

13-5. In this view we see the station and the icehouse to its left. The straight track at right is the Keene Branch looking timetable north (toward Keene). The whistle post is for Elmwood Rd., the first crossing north of the station. (Note: In its day, the M&K never crossed Rte. 202; the highway was not constructed in its present location until ca. 1960, long after the rails had been lifted.) The ball signal is set for the Worcester & Contoocook (two balls). At left are the wye tracks connecting the Nashua and Peterboro tracks. The cars may be boarding cars that were often spotted at this location. Elmwood, ca. mid-1920s. Postcard; Matthew D. Cosgro coll.

13-6. Here is a closeup of the ball signal looking timetable south (toward Nashua) on the Keene Branch. The signal is set for the W&C. The objects visible below the balls are lanterns for use by night. The man in this and the following image is believed to be Howard Goky, Elmwood station agent at the time. Elmwood, 1935. Manahan-Phelps-Mc-Cullough Collection; Hillsborough Hist. Soc.

13-7. The 50,000 gal. Elmwood water tank and pump house were located just timetable east of the Moose Brook Bridge on the W&C Branch. You ask where's the tank's spout? That's easy—there wasn't one. Underground pipes delivered water under head pressure to two standpipes—one on the W&C Branch and one on the Keene Branch, timetable east and north of the station respectively. The tank also supplied water to the station and to the stationmaster's house. After standing unused for a number of years, the tank was retired in 1942 and demolished the following year. With its support timbers pulled, the tank crashed to the ground in ruins amidst a huge swarm of escaping bats! Elmwood, 1935. Manahan-Phelps-McCullough Collection; Hillsborough Hist. Soc.

13-8. Elmwood station, looking at the most-commonly photographed W&C side. The ball signal is just out of the picture to the right. The orderboard masts for the W&C (left) and Keene Branches rise above the station. You cannot see it in the picture, but the Keene Branch track is behind the station. Passenger service is done, and the place looks gloomy. May 14, 1938. Albert G. Hale photo; Walker Trans. Coll/ Historic Beverly.

13-9. Here comes Mogul 1427 with the Nashua–Hillsboro freight. It will cross the diamond, back around the connecting track to the W&C track, and then continue on to Hillsboro, May 14, 1938. Albert G. Hale photo; Walker Trans. Coll./Historic Beverly.

13-10. Mogul 1427 has turned on the wye and is now headed for Hillsboro, May 14, 1938. Albert G. Hale photo; Walker Trans. Coll./Historic Beverly.

13-11. Railfans on an RRE trip, June 29, 1947, are standing on the old Elmwood station site where now only a station sign remains. Their train has returned from Hillsboro on the track at lower right, and fans who wished pictures have detrained. Their train has continued across the diamond onto the stub of the old Peterboro track and now, except for "the thinker," everyone is watching to see the train back over the wye track onto the stub of the old Keene track. That move completed, the train, now headed back to Nashua, would have pulled up to the diamond, picked up lots of happy railfans, and whistled off (see related image in Vol. II, p. 123). All these time-consuming moves were eliminated after Magoon's Curve was commissioned in 1952. Magoon's Curve connected the ends of the Nashua and Hillsboro tracks, permitting continuous operations and the abandonment of all remaining track at Elmwood. Rick Kfoury coll.

Hancock (N35.60)

13-12. The stationmaster and two other men pose for an unknown photographer at the Hancock station. Signs indicate the station offered Western Union Telegraph, Bell Telephone, and American Express service at the time. Notice the Buffalo Scale on the platform—another piece of important station equipage. Undated. Postcard. Benjamin Campbell coll.

13-13. Hancock station, ca. 1930. Louis Benton photo; Benjamin Campbell coll.

13-14. In the western reaches of Hancock, the M&K passed through the Ware family's timberlands. Construction work here included cutting through a large granite ledge, "Ware's Ledge," pictured here, ca. 1878. The cut can be easily accessed and explored from today's Rte. 137. Stereo card, S.A. Putnam (assigned); Benjamin Campbell coll.

Eastview (East Harrisville) (N40.20) and Harrisville (N43.11)

13-15. On a winter's day over 100 years ago these trackmen (Frank Comstock, Alvy Woods, Mike Powers, and Ed Harrington) pause at East Harrisville for their picture. The photographer was probably a family member of one of the men as there was no such thing as a "railfan" in the day. Such pictures that were taken tended to be people centric. The men on the platform appear to be flaggers, doubtless to protect the station crossing (today's Jaquith Rd.). Some type of work was going on nearby. Then there's the dog. Some dogs were "camp followers," attracted by the human activity and excitement of being around the railroad. Some were "railroad smart"—they knew a lot of the men and seemed to understand train schedules and railroad safety rules. East Harrisville, 1906. Benjamin Campbell coll.

13-17. This image, simply labeled "Sweet and crew," shows trackmen posing for their picture on the Nubanusit Brook Bridge (N41.66), roughly halfway between Eastview and Harrisville, 1932. Photogr. unknown; Benjamin Campbell coll.

(*opposite page*)13-16. Here we see a section gang posed for their picture at Eastview station. Eastview was never a train order station, but it had a flag stop signal. Notice the station's name has been changed from East Harrisville to Eastview. This was done to eliminate any confusion with Harrisville proper. The change occurred in 1909, thus dating the image a bit later than the previous image, ca. 1910–20. Postcard, photogr. unknown; Historic Harrisville Archives.

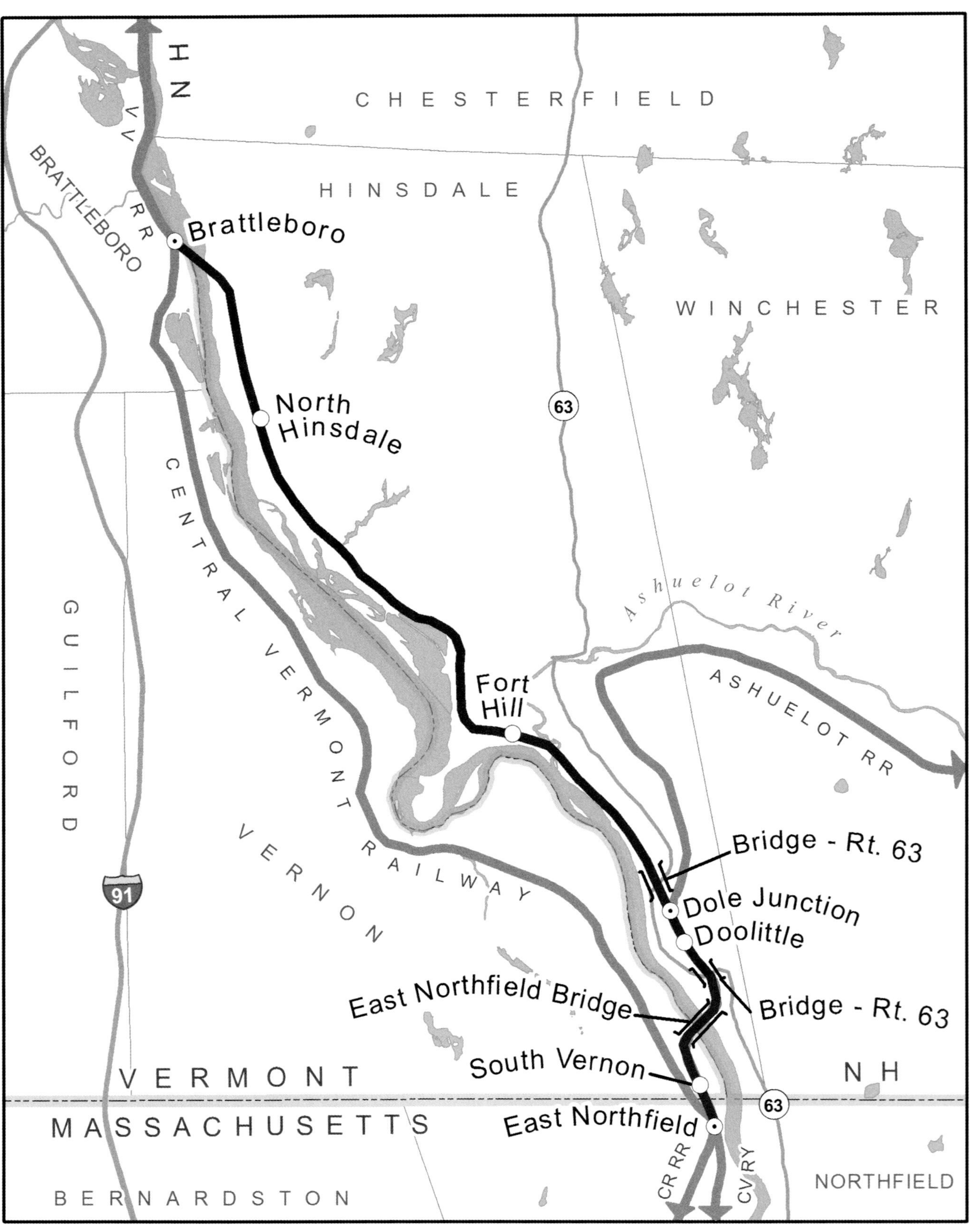

CHESTERFIELD
HINSDALE
WINCHESTER
N H
V V R R
BRATTLEBORO
Brattleboro
North Hinsdale
63
CENTRAL VERMONT RAILWAY
GUILFORD
VERNON
Ashuelot River
ASHUELOT RR
Fort Hill
Bridge - Rt. 63
Dole Junction
Doolittle
East Northfield Bridge
Bridge - Rt. 63
South Vernon
91
VERMONT
MASSACHUSETTS
BERNARDSTON
East Northfield
N H
63
NORTHFIELD
CR RR
CV RY

CHAPTER FOURTEEN

THE CONNECTICUT RIVER RAILROAD EXTENSION
(including late the Fort Hill Branch)

The Connecticut River Railroad (CRRR) was leased in 1893 by the B&M, which operated it as a part of its Connecticut River Main Line. One section of the main line it did not control was an eleven-mile section owned by the Central Vermont (CV) between East Northfield and Brattleboro. Years of friction between the two railroads came to a boiling point in 1910, when the B&M surveyed a new line and secured a charter authorizing the CRRR to build its own line between the two points. The line was built in 1912–1913 by railroad construction firm Holbrook, Cabot, and Rollins (HC&R). It was an example of late railroad building that enjoyed the benefits of relatively modern construction advancements and equipment. Notably, unlike previous railroad construction work, it was photographically documented. It would be the last piece of new railroad construction in the Monadnock Region and one of the last in New England.

Starting at East Northfield, the new line appropriated the first two miles of the Ashuelot Branch, crossing its East Northfield Bridge (S50.52) to the New Hampshire side of the river and continuing to Dole Junction (S51.90). There, it branched off and continued north another 8.5 miles along the Connecticut River through western Hinsdale, before crossing back to the Vermont side of the river at Brattleboro. North of Dole Junction, a single track main line was built with 85-pound rail on gravel ballast. Maximum curvature was 0.4 degrees. Double-arm lower quadrant block signals were installed when the line was built. CTC was installed as far north as Dole Junction in 1964. A long causeway over part of Lake Wantastiquet and the Brattleboro Bridge (S59.26) were the most remarkable features of the line. The bridge consisted of two 250-foot truss spans and five 80-foot deck-plate girder spans—one on the south

approach and four on the north. The line was built to accommodate a second main if future business should ever warrant it (it didn't).

There were now two lines between East Northfield and Brattleboro—the CV on the Vermont side and the CRRR (B&M) on the New Hampshire side of the river. Though this outcome was born of hostility between the B&M and the CV, over the ensuing years, the two roads came to share each other's routes under various operating arrangements. At times the two routes were operated as a double main line with northbound traffic on the New Hampshire side, southbound traffic on the Vermont side. Over the years, though seldom photographed, it was not unusual to see CV trains on the New Hampshire side of the river.

Operations continued normally for many years—until June 1970, when it was discovered the East Northfield Bridge's pier closest to the Vermont shore had shifted to the extent the bridge was taken out of service and never repaired. Through traffic was shifted to the CV line. The B&M's now-former main line from Brattleboro as far south as Doolittle (S50.87) was renamed the Fort Hill Branch and was used by Ashuelot Branch trains to reach Dole Junction. Freight service between Brattleboro and Keene using the Fort Hill and Ashuelot Branches continued until the end of 1983 when the line was abandoned. The line was scrapped in 1984, except for the Brattleboro Bridge, which remains in place to this day.

When the CRRR was extending itself northward through Hinsdale, construction workers sliced through a "Big Sandy Cut" upon which a fort once stood for the protection of early settlers from Indian raids. That is why the Fort Hill Branch—and the Fort Hill station—are so named.

East Northfield Bridge (S50.52)

14-1. Yes indeed, the CV—sharing the B&M's main line through western Hinsdale (as well as about a mile in Walpole), did have a footprint in Cheshire County. Here comes northbound CV Freight 491, drawn by one of CV's Consolidations, crossing the East Northfield Bridge (S50.52) to the New Hampshire side of the river. Trains, let alone CV trains, were rarely photographed on this bridge. It was a long walk to reach either end of the bridge to set up for photography—with no guarantee a train would appear. But intrepid B&M official photographer George H. Hill was there and captured this image for posterity in the waning years of steam, June 18, 1952. B&MRRHS Archives.

Hinsdale, New Hampshire and Fort Hill (S53.85)

14-2. Holbrook, Cabot, and Rollins (HC&R) Marion Model 76 steam shovel at work loading air side-dump cars. It would appear the fireman on the rear platform has made plenty of steam and is relaxing for a few moments, 1912. Benjamin Campbell coll.

14-3. A typical HC&R Forney 0-4-0 engine moving four air side-dump cars along the Connecticut River, 1912. Benjamin Campbell coll.

14-4. HC&R steam pile drivers at work in the Big Sandy Cut, 1912. Benjamin Campbell coll.

14-5. HC&R railroaders (left to right)—Brakeman Raymond, Engineer Leo Dago, Fireman Whalen, Conductor Chymist, Flagman Collins, Operator Auson, and Brakeman Stone, along with a smiling tramp dog, Jack—pose for their pictures with borrowed B&M four-wheel bobber caboose 4906. B&M required a buggy on HC&R trains anytime they went out on B&M track for interchange, July 1912. Photogr. unknown; Brent S. Michiels coll.

14-6. A northbound freight drag approaches the new Fort Hill station (S53.85). Never an important station and with most passenger trains running via the CV, Fort Hill vanished from the timetable in 1929. (*B&M ETT No. 5*, effective Sept. 29, 1929). The Connecticut River is out of the picture to the right. Left of the station, off to the east, the grade of the Ashuelot Branch is visible, 1913. Postcard; B. G. Blodget coll.

14-7. Winter in New England! Looking from atop the Rte. 119 embankment, a train kicks up a cloud of powder snow south of the Brattleboro Bridge (S59.26), North Hinsdale, undated. Scott J. Whitney coll.

CHAPTER FIFTEEN

THE ELECTRIC STREET RAILWAYS
Street Running Under Wires

Keene Electric Railway

The Keene Street Railway Company was chartered in 1887, but due to a lack of funding it was dissolved and rechartered as the Keene Electric Railway (KERy) in 1893. Local funding efforts again failed, and the incorporators sold their interests in the road to Thomas T. Robinson of the Boston Industrial Company in 1900. Construction got underway in the spring of that year and a 6.24-mile main line opened in November, connecting Wheelock Park in West Keene, Central Square, and Marlborough Village. A 2.10-mile extension from the main line to Swanzey Factory opened in 1904. To grow traffic on the extension, the company purchased land on the shore of Wilson Pond, where it developed a recreation park near the end of the line.

Having no connections with any other roads, the KERy was always an isolated system. Financially the road was a marginal operation. Its greatest net profit was $3,662.35 in 1922, its greatest net loss $4,441.89 in 1908. Unfortunately, its meagre results were obtained only by years of deferred maintenance. In 1926, trolley operations were replaced by buses, and the company was sold at the end of 1929 to the Cheshire Transportation Company.

15-1. KERy 45, a Wason, single-truck, ten-bench, open car, is Keene-bound beneath the B&M's Marlborough St. overhead bridge. With the motorman at the controls, the conductor riding the sideboard, and what appears to be a full car, all eyes are on the cameraman. Note part of the Joslin Arch is visible in the image at right. Keene, ca. 1910. Photogr. unknown; Benjamin Campbell coll.

Templeton Street Railway

The Templeton Street Railway (TSRy), organized in 1896, was built in 1899–1900. It commenced operations July 30, 1900, on a 17.87-mile main line from West Gardner Square westward through East Templeton, Templeton Center, and beyond to a point about a half-mile west of the Boston & Albany Railroad's Templeton Station. The carbarn and powerhouse were in East Templeton. In 1901, the road opened a branch from East Templeton to Baldwinville. In the same year, it extended its main line 7.3 miles further west to the Athol Fairgrounds, where it connected with the Athol and Orange Street Railway (A&O). The TSRy purchased land and developed a recreation park at Lake Denison in Winchendon and in 1912 extended its Baldwinville Branch to Winchendon, with a turnout at Lake Denison. In 1913, the road was consolidated with other roads into the Northern Massachusetts Street Railway (NMSRy).

The NMSRy was never profitable. By the end of 1923, the road was in receivership and service was suspended on the Winchendon Branch beyond Baldwinville. In January 1924, a new entity—the Gardner-Templeton Street Railway Company—quickly acquired the remaining assets of the TSRy and continued operations. In December 1925, the company began augmenting service with a bus and all trolley operations were abandoned by the end of 1926. The company continued as a bus line until April 1957, when it was sold to Wilson Bus Lines.

15-2. On the way to Baldwinville, the TSRy crossed the B&M on the Depot Road Bridge and ran right down Main St. in Otter River. This view is looking northward toward Baldwinville. At extreme left is the Otter River Woolen Co., on the site occupied today by Seaman's Paper Co. Postcard, date-stamped Jan. 21, 1909. Harry Aldrich coll.

15-3. TSRy carbarn and the west side of the power plant, East Templeton, ca. 1910. Narragansett Hist. Soc.

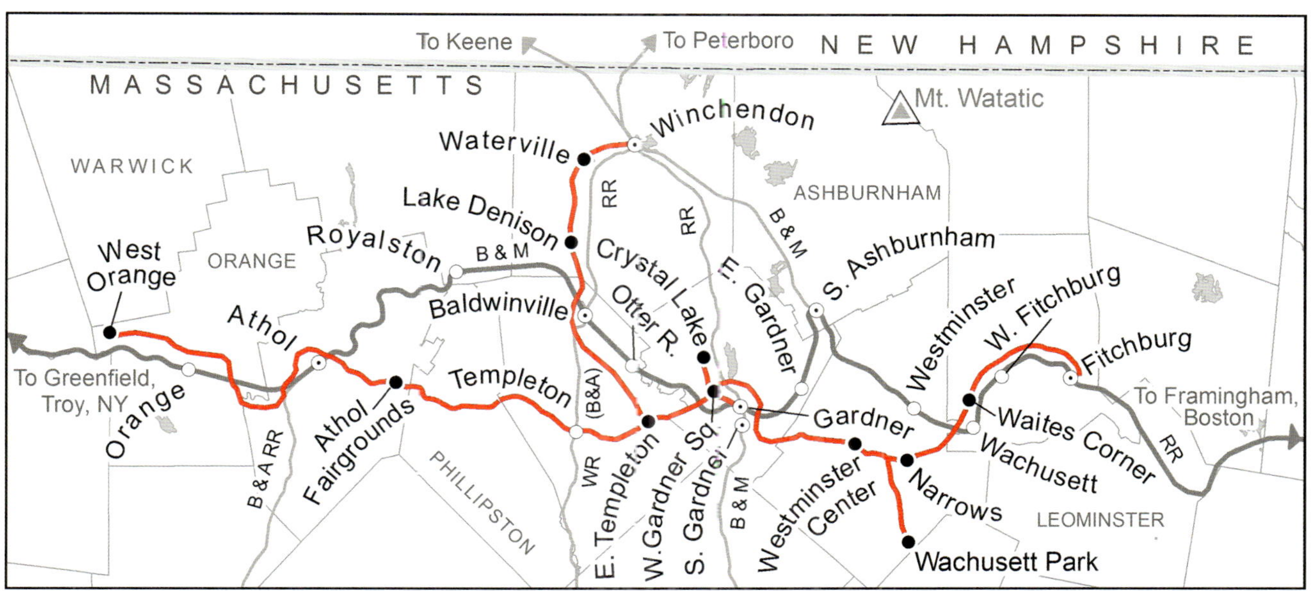

15-4. The TSRy received carload coal from the B&A at Templeton and moved the cars to the power plant in East Templeton. Here is the east side of the plant, showing the coal delivery track. East Templeton, ca. 1910. Narragansett Hist. Soc.

15-5. Map of the Northern Massachuestts Street Railway System

Gardner, Westminster & Fitchburg Street Railway

The Gardner, Westminster & Fitchburg Street Railway (GW&F) was formed in 1899. It absorbed the Gardner Electric Railway and extended it from South Gardner eastward through Westminster to Waite's Corner in the western outskirts of Fitchburg. Service began in 1900. The main line was 15.52 miles in length. The road's carbarn and power plant were located in Westminster, about midway on the line. In Westminster Village, which had been by-passed by the steam roads, the electric cars brought economic prosperity. East of Westminster Village, a two-mile branch left the main line at the Wyman Pond Gatehouse and ran to Wachusett Park, a recreation park and resort at the base of Mount Wachusett. Unfortunately, by 1906 the park was already in decline as the state began to exert more control over recreational use of Wachusett Lake and other public drinking water supplies.

In 1913, the road was consolidated with other roads into the NMSRy system, becoming its GW&F Division. In Fitchburg, the GW&F connected with the Fitchburg & Leominster Street Railway (F&L) at Waite's Corner, and, under an agreement with that road, ran over its tracks into downtown Fitchburg. In season, under a joint ticketing arrangement, the two roads also offered through cars between Wachusett Park in Westminster and Whalom Park in Lunenburg. The F&L was the NMSRy system's only connection with an outside road.

Early on, like most of the street railways, the NMSRy system's traffic was being sapped by the automobile. In addition, the NMSRy was notably plagued by steep grades and severe winter conditions. Unable to generate sufficient income to maintain its infrastructure, the NMSRy filed for bankruptcy in 1923 and the GW&F Division was abandoned the same year. Flanagan Bus Lines assumed the passenger franchise for its routes.

15-6. GW&F employees Ed Rice (left) and Joe Whiting pose somewhere along the line with Wason single-truck, open car 23. Undated. Westminster Hist. Soc.

15-7. Crew and officials pose with single-truck, closed car 10 at the Westminster carbarn and power-house, undated. Westminster Hist. Soc.

15-8. Two GW&F employees with a single-truck, open car, undated. Westminster Hist. Soc.

15-9. Construction of the GW&F through Westminster in 1899–1900 energized business activity in the village. Tracks were laid along the north side of Main St. (old Rte. 2) and for almost a quarter century, the *ding-ding* of streetcar bells would be a familiar sound. However, the streetcar era in Westminster, doomed by the automobile, drew to a close in 1923. In this undated image, a westbound car trundles along Main St. in Westminster Village. Postcard. Westminster Hist. Soc.

15-10. GW&F double-truck, open car 11 displaying a sign for Wachusett Lake, undated. Westminster Hist. Soc.

15-11. In this undated photo, a large group of GW&F employees—many with carnations poked in their button holes—have assembled for a group picture. It must have been an important occasion—even the carbarn cat got into the picture. Westminster Hist. Soc.

15-12. Snowstorms and other severe winter conditions in the NMSRy's territory, all too frequently presented formidable operating challenges and were a factor in the road's early abandonment. Here we find car 25 in a deep snow cut, somewhere out on the line, back in the days of real winters. Westminster Hist. Soc.

PART II

ERRATA AND ADDENDA FOR VOLUMES I AND II

This section includes corrections of errors discovered in Volumes I and II. We regret and apologize for the places where we slipped; they are our goofs, not those of our contributors. We thank those persons (noted below where appropriate) who took a moment to shine light on those places where we strayed. In addition to errata, we present new information pertinent to the first two volumes that we felt warranted sharing with readers.

VOLUME I

Page xii: The date on the camp train photo should be June 28, 1968, not June 8, 1968.

Page 31: In the first column, last paragraph, the term of the V&M lease did not change from 999 years to 99 years at this time. [Thanks to Alden Dreyer for this correction.]

Page 46: In the caption for the top image, the following information should appear after the first sentence: "Note the very high ball signal mast east of the station. At Athol, no balls displayed at the mast head meant that all trains must stop outside of Stop Posts east and west of the depot. One ball displayed gave Springfield, Athol & Northeastern (SA&N) trains exclusive rights to occupy Fitchburg tracks between the stop posts, two balls gave exclusive rights for Fitchburg trains (*Fitchburg Railroad/V&M Div. ETT No. 1*)."

Page 50: There is an error on the M&K map here: the apex of the hairpin turn, shown almost reaching Rte. 9, is too far north. Indeed, the long axis of the hairpin is exaggerated and should only be about half the length shown. The apex is on the Otter Brook Bridge on Branch Road, just north of the junction with Middleton Road in Roxbury. This error has been corrected on the maps reproduced in this volume. [Thanks to Alan Stoops for this correction.]

Page 51: As the much-anticipated opening of the Cheshire-to-Keene line grew near, a letter dated March 29, 1847, that had been written by a correspondent to the *Danvers* (Mass.) *Courier* and previously published by that newspaper, appeared in the April 15, 1847, *Sentinel*. This writer's description of a stagecoach ride from Fitchburg out to Keene is instructive, revealing, and even a bit humorous:

> . . . We arrived at this beautiful town on Saturday night, after a fatiguing ride in the coach from Fitchburg, of *nine hours*, a distance of only 36 miles, having in the previous *two and a half hours* travelled 50 miles by Railroad. This is a fine illustration of the benefits to a traveler of railroad facilities.
>
> At frequent intervals on our route we obtained views of the excavations and embankments of the Cheshire Railroad, which is to pass through Keene, connecting Boston and Fitchburg with Vermont…. We arrived at Keene at half past 7 o'clock, and our gigantic driver brought the coach up at the front of the Cheshire House, where the door was opened by another and a bigger giant, and here we separated from our travelling companions.

Newspaper reporters in the day, without the benefit of photography, wrote more descriptively. Yet still, we can only try to imagine those views seen from the stagecoach windows. Perhaps the views resembled—if you're old enough to remember—how the landscape appeared when the Interstate System was being built in the 1950s–1970s. Railroad construction in the Monadnock Region was photographically undocumented save for the B&M's extension of its CRRR main line through western Hinsdale in 1912.

Page 73: The paragraph at the top of the second column describes the 3820 incorrectly as an E8, rather than an E7. More importantly, however, the 3820 was totaled in the 1954 *Red-wing* accident in Nashua and thus could not have been on this train! Fortunately, thanks to Dick Miller's recent checking the Cheshire Branch timesheet for May 31, 1958, we now know the second unit on this train was actually E7 3816. [Thanks to Dick Miller and Rick Hurst for this correction.]

Page 73: The last paragraph should include the statement, "On December 17, 1959, the ABS System on the branch was retired."

Page 77: In the last paragraph of the left column, the existing text should be replaced from line 7 to the end to read, "In their place, WX-1/XW-2 were established to run between Worcester and Bellows Falls. In 1957, after briefly running as GX-1/XG-2 between Gardner and Bellows Falls, effective Nov. 18, 1957, the trains ran from Fitchburg as FX-1 on Tu-Th-Sa and back as XF-2 on M-W-F. The line between Heywood and Spring St., Winchendon, was taken out of service on Feb. 13, 1958, and abandoned in 1959."

Page 83: The presence of a PennCentral boxcar in the consist in the bottom photo means that the image could not have been captured earlier than 1968. The date in the caption, therefore, would be more accurate as "ca. 1970." [Thanks to Leo Landry for this correction.]

Page 87: The caption for the bottom right image should read: "The east end of the freight house was removed ca. 1957 to make room for this "modern station." The station was raised shortly after this image was taken, Winchendon, Feb. 25, 1970. Photogr. unknown; B&MRRHS Archives."

Page 90: The caption for the bottom image should identify the diesel on 5508 as an E7, not an F7.

Page 102: The bottom left caption should state: "The station is at extreme right." It is not out of the picture.

Page 112: To the left of the water tank in the top photo, note the Keene Gas and Electric (KG&E) Company's gashouse visible beyond. In the day, KG&E received railroad coal from which it manufactured gas. The gas was distributed in the city for heating and lighting.

Page 121: In the bottom image, the individual standing on the ground at left in coveralls is Clyde E. Sessions, MS&N Mechanical Superintendent. [Thanks to Kenton Harrison for identifying this gentleman.]

Page 142: Dwight A. Smith shared with us some additional information about his picture in the middle position on this page. He wrote that the train in this image, ". . . carried a very rare car. Note the second car on the train is a Rutland RR '30' RPO/and all coach.' The 'all coach' part is what is so unusual. Usually, a car with a 15' or 30' RPO also includes a baggage and/or express section." Tom E. Thompson adds that this car was frequently in the *Green Mountain*'s consist.

Page 147: In the first paragraph, the year F. Nelson Blount purchased properties from the B&M is incorrect. The purchase occurred in 1960, not 1961.

Page 148: In the caption for the top photo, we incorrectly stated that 1962 was the only year Steamtown ran a diner on its trains. The diner *Mountaineer* was also used in 1963. [Thanks to Rick Kfoury for this correction.]

Page 152: In the first paragraph, F. Nelson Blount's plane crash is more correctly described as occurring: ". . .in a pasture on Chesham Road in Marlborough." [Thanks to Rick Kfoury and R. Butler for this correction.]

Page 165: Near the end of the second paragraph on the left, the Alco RS2 1500 is described as having a steam boiler inside her short hood. This is incorrect. She was, in fact, the only B&M Alco road switcher not so equipped. [Thanks to L. Kemp for this correction.]

Page 177: Chris Pratt pointed out that it was Sullivan County, NH, that was named in honor of Brigadier General John Sullivan. The Sullivan Railroad (originally chartered as the Sullivan County Railroad) merely adopted the name of the county in which it operated.

Page 182: In the caption on this page, the wheel arrangement for an Atlantic locomotive should, of course, be 4-4-2. [Thanks to C. Pratt for this correction.]

Page 189: The work train in the lower image is at the left, not the right.

Page 191–193: Guilford/B&M 362 on p.191 and 350 on p.192 are GP39s, not GP40s, as they are incorrectly described in their captions. [Thanks to L. Kemp for this correction.] These two locomotives were part of a group of twenty that Guilford acquired when it purchased the D&H in 1984. Richard E. Anderson supplied a 1994 article by Jack Armstrong (*Diesel Era* 7(4):43–46) that explains the service history of this group of diesels on Guilford.

Page 201: The Twitchell House described in the left column was sold for salvage to the F. M. Johnson Lumber Co. of Keene in October 1944.

Page 203: The initial in McLeod's name, at the bottom of the left column, is misplaced. His name is Archibald A. McLeod, not A. Archibald McLeod. And, incidentally, the initial stands for Angus.

VOLUME II

Page vi: This image of the New York Central–Boston & Albany freight house was taken in Winchendon, Massachusetts

Page xviii: The caption for the map on the adjoining page is incorrect. It should read, "The B&M route map as it appeared in 1899, the year before the road leased the Fitchburg Railroad. US National Archives, Washington, DC."

Page xx: In the last paragraph at the bottom of the left column, "United States Railroad Authority" should be "United States Railroad Administration."

Page 24: The streetcar shown on the Fitchburg flat at Ashburnham is actually an electric car, not a horsecar. Kenton Harrison astutely pointed out that there are controller levers at both ends of the car and that the man standing on the left end of the car is resting a hand on one of them. Furthermore, Kenton noted that by 1895, the building of horsecars had already ended.

Page 32: In the third paragraph of the right column, the following sentence should appear after the September 3, 1874, citation from the *Transcript*: "BB&G shareholders approved the merger at a Special Meeting in Worcester September 26, 1874. Their action checkmated. . . ." [We thank Richard Hurst for sharing a copy of the original notice announcing the results of this meeting, recently discovered in the B&MRRHS Archives in Lowell, Massachusetts.]

Page 36: In the third paragraph of the left column, the newspaper credited should be the *Worcester Daily Spy*, which carried a more detailed account of the wreck than the *New York Times*.

Page 37: More on passenger service between Worcester and Peterboro at midcentury: Picking up with *B&M ETT No. 4* (April 28, 1929), there were two daily round trips. Service dropped to one daily round trip effective with *ETT No. 20* (April 26, 1936) and continued at this frequency until the end of service in 1953, except that Sunday service disappeared from the *ETT*s starting with No. 50 (April 30, 1950).

Page 38: In the second paragraph of the right column, we stated that the line between Heywood and Winchendon was taken out of service in April 1958. However, recently discovered Bulletin Orders reveal the out-of-service date was actually a bit earlier—on February 13, 1958.

Page 53: The bottom photo shows GP7 1563, *not* 1573.

Page 57: The caption at the bottom of the preceding page is incorrect. It should read: "Train 8118/Mogul 1457 approaching Noone, 1952. George C. Corey photo."

Page 58: In the caption for the top left photo on this page, the sponsoring organization for the 1955 New Haven RDC special over the Peterboro Branch was the New England Railfan Association, not a chapter of the National Railroad Historical Society. [Thanks to William T. Clynes for this correction.]

Page 59: The caption for the bottom photo is incorrect. It should read: "Train 8118/Mogul 1457 approaching Noone. That is MP51 visible to the rear of the train. 1952. Stanwood K. Bolton photo." [Thanks to L. Kemp for this correction.]

Page 65: The caption for the top photo incorrectly describes the photographer as "unknown." The image was taken by Carlton Parker.

Page 73: In the caption for the middle photo on this page, the sponsoring organization for the 1955 New Haven RDC special over the Peterboro Branch was the New England Railfan Association, not a chapter of the National Railroad Historical Society. [Thanks to William T. Clynes for this correction.]

Page 75: While we discussed the deadly accident at Nahor October 16, 1929, Larry Kemp shared a newspaper clip from his files that described an earlier, lesser-known accident at Nahor. Whoever said lightening never strikes in the same place twice? It happened in the early evening of November 17, 1926. The nearly brand-new Osgood Bradley gas-electric motorcar 186 and its trailer on Train 8115, met a light engine about 100 feet west of Nahor Crossing on the Hancock Road. The crewmen on 8115 were badly injured. The crew on the light engine and sectionmen who were aboard 8115 traveling to their homes (probably boarding cars) near Elmwood were shaken up and bruised, but otherwise uninjured. A single passenger escaped uninjured (*Peterboro Transcript* Nov. 17, 1926). The 186 was considerably damaged but was repaired and went on to have a long service life.

Page 87: In the caption for the lower image, we slipped up on the date of the Hillsboro Bridge fire. The bridge was torched by an arsonist and destroyed on Oct. 30, 1983.

Page 104: There is an error on the M&K map here: the apex of the hairpin turn, shown almost reaching Rte. 9, is too far north. Indeed, the long axis of the hairpin is exaggerated and should only be about half the length shown. The apex is on the Otter Brook Bridge on Branch Road, just north of the junction with Middleton Road in Roxbury. This error has been corrected on the maps reproduced in this volume. [Thanks to Alan Stoops for this correction.]

Page 121: In addition to the duties of Train 275 from Nashua to Keene described in the left column, the duties of the train's other side are also described in B&M Symbol Book No. 5, January 1, 1915:

No. 276–*Ex. Sun.* Handles from Keene, merchandise cars for diverging route via Elmwood and for Nashua, U.S., and local cars for points between Keene and Nashua. Loads and unloads L.C.L. freight at all stations Keene to Nashua, U.S. Handles cars for and from, and does station switching for all points Keene to Elmwood. Fill to rating at Keene and Elmwood with southbound cars from Worcester & Hillsboro Branch at Elmwood. At Greenfield, take rush shipments for points on M&M Branch via Milford. Takes ice shipments from Whitings ice track Greenfield. Takes at Milford all cars made up on track No. 10. Connects at Keene, Elmwood and Milford with way-freight service via connecting divisions. Carries passengers.

Depending on traffic conditions, an extra would sometimes follow 275 Nashua to Elmwood and precede 276 back to Nashua.

Page 126: The South Bennington station shown in the top photo was eventually sold to a private party and moved to a site in Hancock. There, it slowly deteriorated until it burned in June 2019. [Thanks to L. Kemp for this correction.]

Page 131: *B&M ETT No. 15* (Sept. 24, 1933) shows Eastview dropped as a passenger stop. Discontinuance of passenger service here turned out to be a prescient move on the railroad's part, as the disastrous flooding that would follow on Jan. 9, 1934, ended forever all passenger service between Elmwood and Keene. The station building shown in the bottom photo was razed Sept. 26, 1935. The stationmaster's house, located on Jaquith Road next to the site of the former station, is now a private residence. Built by the B&M in 1896, it is listed on the National Register of Historic Places. The building has been extensively renovated and is no longer recognizable as a railroad structure.

Page 132: The third sentence in the left column should be changed to read: "As the railroad grade was well below the town, everything was drayed to and from the station." [Thanks to L. Kemp for this correction.]

Page 132: The date given in the caption for the top photo is incorrect. It should read "1922".

Page 134: Ever wonder how West Harrisville became "Chesham?" The name change was requested by a George B. Chase, Esq. of Boston, who had built "a fine villa at nearby Stone Pond [*sic*]," two-and-a-half-miles south on the Dublin–Marlborough line. His request was met with no opposition and the change was made, effective October 27, 1886. "Chesham," a contraction of **Ch**ase and **Esq**., would presumably have been the station Chase used when traveling to and from his home at Stone Pond. At about the same time, the post office name was also changed—from Pottersville to Chesham (*Sentinel* Oct. 27, 1886).

Page 135: In the top image, the small building at left center was a butcher shop owned by William H. McGrath.

Page 137: The caption for the top right photo is inaccurate. The image was taken ca. 1930, and the photographer was Louis Benton.

Page 139: Under the discussion of Roxbury Crossing, the name of the quarry should be "Bodwell Quarry" (see notes by Henry Taves in *B&M Bull.* Vol. 20(2):5).

Page 143: In the right column, the numbers of the Budd cars purchased by the Wilton Scenic were RDC-1 BC-15 and RDC-3 BC-30. [Thanks to L. Kemp for this correction.]

Page 147: The last two sentences of the paragraph ending at the top of the right column, should be corrected as follows: "Double-arm lower quadrant block signals were installed when the line was built. CTC was installed as far north as Dole Junction in 1964." [Thanks to Alden Dreyer for this correction.]

Page 155: The second paragraph, which begins at the bottom of the left column gives an incorrect distance between Springfield and Sherbrooke. It should read: "Upon completion of the CRRR Extension, the B&M controlled a continuous 267-mile line of road from Springfield, Massachusetts, to Sherbrooke, Quebec, except for seventeen miles—fourteen miles between Windsor and White River Junction, and three miles between Lennoxville and Sherbrooke—over which it had trackage rights." We should have caught this one, especially since we had the same mileage correct at two earlier occurrences in the book! [Thanks to S. Whitney for this correction.]

Page 156: At the top of the right column, "United States Railroad Authority" should be "United States Railroad Administration."

Page 156–157: The view at the bottom of these pages is timetable *southward*, not northward (i.e., looking from Hinsdale, NH, towards the Vermont shore). [Thanks to D. Manson for this correction.]

Page 157: On the advice of Alden Dreyer, the last sentence of the paragraph that ends at the top of the left column should be deleted.

Page 184: In the left column, we incorrectly stated that beyond Baldwinville, the TSRy's Winchendon Branch "ran generally in Rte. 202 to Waterville." Rte. 202 as we know it today did not exist in 1912 when the Winchendon Branch was constructed. Leaving Baldwinville, the road ran in Elm Street, to a point where it swung over the B&M on a steel girder bridge, thence over private land about four miles to Main Street in Winchendon, thence in Main Street into the village of Waterville (*Forty-fourth Annual Rept. of the Board of Railroad Commissioners,* Comm. of Mass., Jan. 1913, page 336). In 1923—after only eleven years of operation—service on the Winchendon Branch beyond Baldwinville ended. A section of the old roadbed was appropriated for Rte. 202 when it was built.

Page 185: In the caption for the bottom image, freight motor 0510 is incorrectly identified as being from the Boston Elevated Street Railway. It was built in 1913 by Osgood Bradley for the Boston and Worcester Street Railway, which sold it the following year to the Northern Massachusetts Street Railway (Cummings, O. R. 1975. *Trolleys Along the Turnpike,* pages 75–76 and 86).

Only recently delivered from its builder (Alco) in June 1948, B&M RS2 1500 was placed into service on the Fitchburg Division, where it would spend most of its life. One of its first assignments was in fact on the freights between Worcester and Bellows Falls. Here the 1500 is on the Cheshire Branch, bringing WX-1 onto granite arch bridge B83.24 over the South Branch of the Ashuelot River in Troy, NH. Visible at right is the old Keene Road, discontinued after the completion of Route 12 in 1945. The breathtaking view of the Grand Monadnock is gone today, snuffed out by forest growth along the line. This scene, from ca. June 1948, was captured on Jim Dufour's Cheshire Railroad model layout, Sept. 2022. Jim Dufour photo.

PART III

CONSOLIDATED INDEX FOR VOLUMES I–III

Note: **bold** page numbers denote major chapters

This is the remote, three-span, 210-foot, steel girder Otter River Bridge (B72.55) built by the B&M and the Army Engineers in 1940. The view shows two of the bridge's three spans, looking upstream from the rubble remains of the bridge's predecessor, built by the Fitchburg Railroad in 1881–1882 (see map and discussion in Chapter 1). We thank Dorothy Daigle Gallant of Baldwinville for sharing her image of this rarely-photographed bridge, west of Baldwinville, Jan. 14, 2023.